Diverse Divorce

18 SITUATION STORIES FOR USE WITH CHILDREN OF DIVORCE

WRITTEN BY
Lisa Lawmaster Hess

ILLUSTRATED BY
Marie Garafano

ABOUT THE AUTHOR

Lisa Lawmaster Hess

Lisa Lawmaster Hess is the author of the book *Acting Assertively* as well as numerous newspaper and magazine articles. An elementary school counselor, Lisa often writes on educational topics, but has also published articles on decorating, theatre, and wedding planning. She resides in York, PA with her husband and daughter. Although she's lived in Pennsylvania for more than 20 years, she still considers New Jersey home.

Published by **mar*co products, inc**.
1443 Old York Road
Warminster, PA 18974
1-800-448-2197

ISBN: 1-57543-127-0

Printed in the U.S.A.

Acknowledgments

This book would never have seen the light of day if it weren't for a lot of people. Tremendous thanks go to Sharon Whittle, my principal, who supported the idea of offering groups for children of divorce. Thanks also go to the parents and teachers at East York Elementary School, who graciously shared their kids with me even when it was inconvenient for them to do so.

There would be no book if it weren't for those kids—the students in my drop-in groups—who have taught me more about divorce, love, and resiliency than I could read in any textbook and who trusted me enough to share their experiences, feelings, and insights with me and with each other.

I am also grateful to Trinka Enell at The Institute of Children's Literature, who kept me on task and taught me that I could write fiction; to the members of my writers group—Anne, Jackie, Julie, Kim, Lori, Maggie, Maria, Mike, Nancy, and Shawn—who read each story and helped me make it better; to Judy and Laurie, who read and reread, and sent me funny e-mails just when I needed them; to Barb, Mary Beth, and Sandy, who gave me an educator's perspective honestly, yet gently; and to Amy and Shannon, who took care of my child so I could have time to get the stories out of my head and onto the page.

And always, to my parents, my sister, my husband, and my daughter, whose generosity and belief in me help me to make my dreams reality.

Contents

Introduction

I used to have a literal interpretation of the term *children of divorce*. But after 17 years as a school counselor, I've learned that the boundaries for this group are blurry. These children may have lost a parent not only to divorce, but to marital separation or the breakup of a relationship that did not include marriage. One parent may be incarcerated, disinterested, or gone for good. Parental figures aren't limited to mothers and fathers. They can also be boyfriends, girlfriends, stepparents, and grandparents. The children of all of these relationships struggle with many of the same issues, regardless of the marital status of their parents.

This book is for all of these children. Each chapter features a different child adjusting to a changing family and coping with the feelings that go along with these changes. I was certainly inspired by my students. But for reasons of confidentiality, you won't find any of their stories in the pages of this book, despite their pleas and reassurances that they'd be happy to help. I'm certain, however, that pieces of each of their stories, personalities, and insights are interwoven throughout the book.

What you will find is 18 protagonists (some with siblings, many without) dealing with 18 different situations. Eight of the situations are most appropriate for younger children and 10 are most appropriate for older children. My hope is that all of *your* kids can find something to relate to.

While upper elementary and middle school students can certainly read and digest the stories on their own, I envisioned this book as a set of stories for kids to read and discuss with a counselor or teacher in a small-group or classroom setting or, perhaps, at home with a parent. Used in this manner, all of these stories are appropriate for elementary and middle school children. The summary at the beginning of each chapter can help you decide whether a particular story will be useful for your group.

One of the reasons I run groups for children of divorce is to help them feel less alone. I hope this book accomplishes the same thing.

Getting Started

All kids, regardless of their family constellation, need to know they are safe, they are loved, and they will be cared for. Children of divorce need to be reassured that the divorce is not their fault, they are not responsible for their parents' actions, and that their parents remain their parents, no matter what. Keeping these needs in mind can help leaders guide any group discussion, regardless of the direction it may take.

If possible, groups should be composed of children who have *chosen* to participate, rather than those who have been volunteered. However, a child should not be eliminated because of an outside referral. The ideal group size depends upon the age of the members and the comfort level of the group leader. Generally speaking, younger children need smaller groups (no more than five or six participants). Working with a co-facilitator can allow you to run larger groups while still giving children the individual attention they need. At least one leader should have some familiarity with typical reactions to loss, as children of divorce often need reassurance that what they're feeling is normal.

Groups can meet as often as every day or as infrequently as once a month. It is usually best if the leader is an adult who is comfortable facilitating a discussion, and even better if that adult has some background in counseling and/or child development.

Using The Stories

How you choose and use the stories is up to you. The stories can be read in any order, though Erin's story *(When Irish Eyes Aren't Smiling)* may be a good one to start with. Found at the beginning of the section for older children, this story introduces the concept of a group for children of divorce. If the members of your group are old enough, you may wish to have them select the stories they'd like to read. The whole group can focus on one story at a time. Or subgroups may discuss different stories.

Most of the stories are suitable for all readers, regardless of the specifics of their family situation. A few deal with more mature themes, however, so you will want to read the summary at the beginning of each story before using it with your group.

The stories can be read aloud at meetings or reproduced and given to the participants to read ahead of time so that everyone comes prepared for discussion. Groups meeting less often than once a week should probably read the stories between meetings in order to maximize discussion time.

The details of the post-story discussions depend entirely on the needs of your kids. Although discussion questions are included with each chapter, general questions like those below will be appropriate for all of the stories.

- Have you ever had feelings like (INSERT THE NAME OF THE MAIN CHARACTER)?
- Have you ever been in a situation like the one in the story?
- Do you think other kids might feel the way the kids in the story felt? Why or why not?
- What advice would you give the character in the story?

These questions are just suggestions. Feel free to stray from them and to take advantage of detours and personal connections that help children relate the stories to their own experiences.

What's more important than the discussion itself is the atmosphere you create. When a discussion revolves around topics as personal as family events, it's important that kids feel safe sharing private thoughts and emotions. I've found that if group members are given the freedom to pass when they do not wish to share, along with the promise that their comments will remain within the confines of the group, the agenda takes care of itself and kids feel free to discuss their honest reactions and make the personal connections that are so invaluable.

As you plan your group meetings, bear in mind that no matter how thoroughly you prepare, there will be detours and surprises. Much of what the children remember will be things they discover themselves in conversations that have departed dramatically from the discussion you had in mind. Remember, sometimes we just have to sit back and let them teach each other. In the process, we often learn something, too.

Happy reading, and best wishes to you and your amazing groups!

Lisa Lawmaster Hess

Diverse Divorce Stories For Young Children

What's In A Name?

(Concern Over An Argument Between A Parent And Stepparent)

SUMMARY:

In Kaitlin O'Brien's family, everyone usually gets along. So when her mother and stepfather have an argument at the dinner table, Kaitlin is left feeling upset and confused. Although Kaitlin plans to talk with her teacher at recess, her best friend Brigid convinces her to talk with Mrs. Donovan, the school counselor.

POST-STORY DISCUSSION QUESTIONS:

Some of the following questions can be answered with a "yes" or "no." In these cases, the child giving an answer should explain his/her reasons.

1. In this story, Kaitlin talked with Brigid and Mrs. Donovan about her feelings. Who helps *you* when you're upset?
2. Was there ever a time when you tried to stay busy to make the time pass quickly? If so, when?
3. What's on your *remedies* list?
4. Is your guidance counselor anything like Mrs. Donovan?
5. Mrs. Donovan told Kaitlin that what she was feeling was normal. Do you agree?
6. Even though nothing has changed, why do you think Kaitlin feels better after talking with Mrs. Donovan?
7. Why do you think Kaitlin wants to be a Fitzgerald?

FOLLOW-UP ACTIVITY:

Materials Needed:

- ☐ 4" x 6" unruled index card and crayons or markers for each child
- ☐ Stickers (optional)

After reading the story and discussing the questions, distribute an index card and crayons or markers to each child. Remind the children that Kaitlin wanted a different name. She wanted to be a Fitzgerald. Ask the children if they have ever wanted to change their names (first or last) for any reason. Then ask the children to create name tags, using the name they chose for themselves. Explain that if they don't want a different name, they may write down the name they have. Tell the children how much time they have to complete the name tags. When the allotted time has elapsed, ask each child to tell what name he/she chose and why.

What's In A Name?

"**Kaitlin?" my teacher called.** "Would you come here for a minute?"

I stood up and walked over to Mr. Masters' desk. He's my second-grade teacher, and he's awesome. When my best friend, Brigid, and I found out we'd be in his class, we did cartwheels from my front yard to my back yard. And last week, when we were on spring break, I couldn't wait to come back to school.

As soon as I got to Mr. Masters' desk, I knew what he wanted. I knew because he was holding my spelling homework. I'm a good speller, so I knew I'd spelled all the words right. Except …

Mr. Masters was pointing to the name at the top of my paper.

"What's going on?" he whispered. "You haven't called yourself *Kaitlin Marie O'Brien Fitzgerald* since the first week of school. Is everything all right?"

I looked around the room, then shook my head. "Can I talk with you at recess?" I asked.

"Sure," Mr. Masters said. "Will you be okay until then?"

I nodded. "Thanks, Mr. Masters."

I went back to my seat and started on my morning work. Maybe if I stayed busy, the time until recess would pass more quickly.

At 10:30, our school counselor, Mrs. Donovan, came in to teach a class. She was wearing a sweatshirt with lots of different faces on it, and she told us that we were going to talk about all the different kinds of feelings we have. Then we made a list of *feeling words*, and another list of *remedies*—things to do when we feel miserable. When the recess bell rang, Brigid said we should add *recess* to the *remedies* list. Mrs. Donovan laughed.

Brigid came over to my desk. "Maybe you should talk with Mrs. Donovan," she said.

"About what?" I replied.

"About whatever's making *you* miserable. You haven't smiled all morning," Brigid answered.

I looked around to make sure no one was listening. Then I said, "Mom and Richard had a big fight last night. Right at the dinner table, too, in front of Rachel and me."

"Wow!" Brigid said. "They never fight."

"I know," I replied. "It's so weird! I'm scared, Bridge."

"Hey, Mrs. Donovan," Brigid called. "May Kaitlin and I talk with you?"

I slid down in my seat, wishing I could crawl into my desk.

"Sure," Mrs. Donovan answered, tilting her head to one side. "Only it looks as though Kaitlin doesn't want to talk."

"It's just that I was supposed to talk with my teacher now," I said. I looked at Mr. Masters, hoping he would get me out of this. But he just smiled.

"It's fine, Kaitlin," Mr. Masters said. "We can talk another time."

"Come on," Brigid said, pulling me out of my chair. "I'll go to Mrs. D's office with you."

I was really mad at Brigid at first, but by the time we got to Mrs. Donovan's office, I thought maybe talking with her wasn't such a bad idea after all.

The office wasn't very big, but there was a lot to look at. All the walls had posters on them, and one wall had a big window with flowered curtains. There were piles and piles of paper on the desk. Mr. Masters would make us stay in from recess if our desks looked like that.

"Now, Kaitlin," Brigid said, "whatever you tell Mrs. D. stays private. Unless you're in some kind of danger."

"How do you know so much about this?" I asked. Brigid shrugged. "I've seen her before, remember?"

"Oh, yeah," I said, remembering Brigid visited her office last year when Susan Peters was being really mean to her. Mrs. Donovan had helped Brigid figure out what to do.

Mrs. Donovan sat at the table with us. "Kaitlin, you looked so sad in class. Are you girls having trouble getting along?"

"Oh, no," I said. "It's about my parents."

"Oh," Mrs. Donovan replied. "Do you want Brigid to stay, or would you prefer she go to recess?"

"Oh, she can stay," I answered. "I tell her everything, anyway."

Once I started talking, it all came pouring out. I told Mrs. Donovan all about my parents' divorce, my mom marrying Richard, and how everyone usually got along great. I even told her how much I wanted to be a Fitzgerald, like everyone else in my house. Then I told her about the fight.

"And they never argue," Brigid interrupted.

"Does this mean they're going to get a divorce?" I asked.

"No, Kaitlin," Mrs. Donovan said. "All married couples argue. It's normal. And a lot of kids whose parents are divorced worry about having to go through it again. That's normal, too."

"Really?" I asked.

"Really," Mrs. Donovan said. "Have you talked with your parents?"

I shook my head. "No. I'm afraid to do that."

"Who's easier to talk with?" Mrs. Donovan asked. "Your mom or your stepdad?"

"Definitely my mom," I answered.

"Okay," Mrs. Donovan said. "You be you and I'll be your mom. Tell me how you're feeling."

We practiced for a long time. Brigid and I took turns being me. At first, Mrs. Donovan pretended to be a perfect mom, listening carefully and telling me everything would be okay. Just as I thought this talking was easy, Mrs. Donovan made it harder by pretending to be a mom in a grouchy mood. That was my favorite part. But Mrs. Donovan wasn't very good at being grouchy, and we all ended up giggling.

After we practiced, Mrs. D. asked me if I felt ready to talk with my mom.

I nodded.

"I'll make sure she does," Brigid said.

Mrs. D. laughed. "I think Kaitlin has it under control," she said. "Besides, it's *her* family. *She* has to be the one to solve this."

Then Mrs. D. looked at me and smiled. "Kaitlin, will you come back and let me know how things work out?"

"Sure," I said. "Thanks, Mrs. Donovan."

On the way back to our classroom, Brigid and I were both sort of quiet.

"Are you still mad at me?" Brigid finally asked.

"No," I paused. "I was at first. But I wouldn't have gone by myself, and all that practicing really helped."

"Yeah," Brigid said. "I did that with her when I was too scared to talk with my mom."

"But your mom's so cool!" I said.

"Not when I'm in trouble! Besides, Mrs. D. has this way of making you feel like you're normal, even when you feel weird."

I laughed, "Yeah, you're right. I do feel better, even though nothing's different."

When we got back to the classroom, everyone was working on their autobiographies for Spring Open House. I thought for a moment, then picked up my pencil.

"My name is Kaitlin Marie O'Brien," I wrote. "My parents are divorced. Most of the time, I live with my mom; my half sister, Rachel; and my stepdad, Richard. They're all Fitzgeralds. Someday I want to be a Fitzgerald, too."

Weddings Are Fishy Business

(Anxiety Over A Remarriage)

SUMMARY:

Michael's father is getting married again, and Michael is not happy about it. He's sure that everything will change. He's not so sure about his soon-to-be stepmother, Jennifer, who hates camping, fishing, and video games. A conversation with his father and a surprise from Jennifer help make the wedding day a little less painful for Michael.

POST-STORY DISCUSSION QUESTIONS:

Some of the following questions can be answered with a "yes" or "no." In these cases, the child giving an answer should explain his/her reasons.

1. Are all stepmothers like the one in *Cinderella*? How do you know?
2. Sarah's worried that it's "bad luck" for the groom to see the bride on the day of the wedding. Do you think she's right?
3. Michael and his sister have very different feelings about this wedding. Why do you think this is so?
4. Can you be friends with someone who doesn't like the same things you like? Could you get along with a stepparent whose tastes are different from yours?
5. If you had a stepmom or stepdad, would you want to call her *Mom* or call him *Dad*?
6. When Michael's dad raised his eyebrows at him, Michael knew what his dad wanted. Do your parents have "a look" that tells you what they want even before they say anything?
7. How do your parents cheer you up when you are unhappy?

FOLLOW-UP ACTIVITY:

Materials Needed:

- ☐ Construction paper or cardboard, scissors, and markers or crayons for each child
- ☐ Arts and crafts scraps such as beads, feathers, foam shapes, tissue paper, fabric scraps, sequins, raffia, etc.

Place the arts and crafts scraps on a table each child can reach. Distribute scissors, construction paper or cardboard, and markers or crayons to each child. Remind the children that Sarah was worried that if her dad saw Jennifer before the wedding, it would be bad luck. Then tell them that people sometimes carry a good luck charm, hoping they will avoid having bad luck. A rabbit's foot or four-leaf clover may be used as an example. Tell the children to create a good luck charm from the materials on the table. Tell the children how much time they have to complete the activity. When the allotted time has elapsed, ask each child the following questions:

1. For whom did you make the good luck charm?
2. Why did you choose to make the charm for that person?
3. How did you decide which materials to use to decorate your good luck charm?

Weddings Are Fishy Business

My dad's getting married today. His new wife's name is Jennifer. She's tall with brown hair and dark brown eyes, and my dad keeps calling her *honey* and kissing her and stuff. She doesn't like video games or camping or fishing.

We're in one of the Sunday School rooms in the basement of the church getting ready for the wedding. My goofy sister, Sarah, is twirling around in front of the mirror, wearing a frilly purple dress that goes all the way to the floor. She's humming *Here Comes The Bride* and pretending to throw rose petals.

I take off my sweatshirt and put on the white shirt that I have to wear for the wedding. Dad already tucked the tie under the collar and buttoned the little buttons that hold it down. I hate getting dressed up!

"Sarah, don't you get it?" I ask. "We're getting a new mother. Why are you so happy?"

Sarah puts her hands on her hips and flashes me her "you're so dumb" look.

"We are *not* getting a new mother, Michael. We *have* a mother. Jenn will be our *stepmother*," Sarah tells me for the millionth time.

"Yeah. Like in *Cinderella,*" I mutter.

Sarah rolls her eyes and goes back to twirling and humming. I hope I'm not that goofy when I'm eight.

"Sarah?" Dad calls as he pokes his head into the room. "Jenn wants to see you for a minute."

Sarah spins past me to the door. "Daddy, you aren't supposed to see Jenn before the wedding," she says anxiously.

"I didn't see her, Sarah," Dad reassures her. "The hair stylist told me."

"Oh, good!" Sarah says. "I wouldn't want you and Jenn to have bad luck." Sarah hugs Dad, then dances through the doorway.

"Girls are so weird," I say to Dad.

Dad laughs. "She's just excited. A wedding's a big deal."

"If you're a girl," I grumble. "I don't want a stepmother."

Dad sighs and sits down next to me. I know he's tired of having this conversation. "Mikey," he says, "Jenn and I have been together for two years. Things aren't going to be that different."

"Yeah, I know," I answer. "But now she'll be there all the time. Dad, she doesn't even like video games!"

"Then she doesn't have to play them," Dad says. "But *we* still can."

"She hates camping," I tell him, "and fishing."

"So once in a while, she and Sarah can have a girls' weekend while you and I have a guys' weekend. We can pitch a tent at the lake and fish all weekend."

I look at him, surprised, "You'd do that?"

"Of course I would," Dad says.

"Will Jennifer let you?"

Now Dad laughs. "Mikey, Jenn's going to be my wife, not my boss. Do you think I'd marry someone who doesn't understand how important you and Sarah are?"

I shrug. "I guess not. It's just that it won't be the same."

"No, it won't," Dad agrees, "but it can be pretty awesome if you let it."

"Do I have to call her *Mom*?"

"Not if you don't want to."

"Do I have to clean up and use manners and stuff like that?" I ask.

"Not any more than before," Dad answers.

Sarah bursts into the room, tossing her hair back and forth. "Look at the barrettes Jenn gave me! They match my dress. And they're all sparkly!" Sarah stops bouncing around and looks at me.

"Michael!" she scolds. "You're aren't even dressed yet! And your shirt's all wrong."

"No, it's not," I say. But when I look down at my shirt, I see it's buttoned crooked. The purple tie that matches Sarah's dress is hanging untied down the front of my shirt. And I still have my sweatpants on.

"Sarah," Dad says, "why don't you see if Jenn needs any help?"

Sarah pirouettes out of the room and I rebutton my shirt and finish getting dressed. Dad's knotting my tie when Sarah prances back in.

"Michael, Jenn wants to see you," Sarah announces.

"Do I have to?" I ask Dad.

Dad raises his eyebrows, so I go out the door, shuffle down the hall, and knock on the door of the Bride's Room.

"Come in," Jennifer calls.

I open the door. Jennifer's standing there looking like one of Sarah's princess dolls. I hate her for a minute, then I look at her face. I've never seen anyone look so happy in real life.

"Hi, Mike," she giggles. "I can't sit down in this dress. Isn't that silly?"

I wonder why anyone would buy a dress she can't sit down in, but I don't ask.

"I have something for you," she says.

Jennifer hands me a box wrapped in silver paper and tied with a purple ribbon. Inside it is a pin shaped like a fish. It looks just like the bass Dad caught at the lake last summer, only it's a lot smaller, and it has a sort of button that goes over the pin in the back.

"It's a tie tack," Jennifer tells me. "I thought you might want to wear it today. I know how much you hate the purple tie, so I thought this might make it a little better."

I look at her for a minute, wanting to ask her if this was Dad's idea. Then I decide it doesn't really matter.

"Thank you," I say, twirling the button part around and trying to figure out what to do with it.

"Here," Jennifer says, "let me help."

Just as Jennifer pokes the pin through my tie, Sarah bursts through the door again.

"It's time! Come on, Michael!" Sarah exclaims.

I start for the door, then look back at Jennifer.

"Thanks, Jenn. Happy wedding," I tell her.

I follow Sarah to the chapel and stand beside my dad. When I show him the fish pin, he smiles and shakes his head.

So it wasn't his idea after all. I wonder if Jenn has any more good ideas.

Goodbye, Old Life

(Financial Difficulties Require Moving In With A Relative)

SUMMARY:

When Jasmine's parents get divorced, Jasmine's mother can't afford her own place. So they have to move in with relatives. As they wait for the moving van to arrive and Jasmine finishes packing up her room, she hangs on to an old friend and wonders about what will happen next.

POST-STORY DISCUSSION QUESTIONS:

Some of the following questions can be answered with a "yes" or "no." In these cases, the child giving an answer should explain his/her reasons.

1. Have you ever had to move? How did moving make you feel?
2. Have you ever stayed at a relative's house? Was it fun or not?
3. Why does it matter to Jasmine that she can't walk to kindergarten with Rosa any more?
4. Where do you think Jasmine will put her things at Aunt Carol's? Where do you think she and her mom will stay while they are there?
5. Did you have a special toy when you were little? What was it? Do you have one now? Is it the same one?

FOLLOW-UP ACTIVITY:

Materials Needed:

- ☐ Shoe box or empty cereal box for each child
- ☐ Decorating materials such as construction paper, wallpaper scraps, contact paper, markers, crayons, paints, glue sticks, glitter, stickers, etc.

Distribute a box to each child. Tell the children to decorate their box as if it was a suitcase or trunk. Then remind the children that Jasmine wouldn't leave home without her blanket. Tell the children how much time they have to complete the activity. When the allotted time has elapsed, have the children answer the following questions:

1. What would you put into your suitcase if you were moving?
2. What would you put into your suitcase if you were going to visit a parent you don't live with all the time?
3. What would you put into your suitcase if you were going to a sleepover?

Goodbye, Old Life

I tossed a pink T-shirt into my suitcase, then plopped down onto the bed beside it. Pulling Boo out of my backpack, I wrapped myself in his soft blue flannel. My sheets were in a pile on the floor next to the bed. My comforter and pillow were already packed, along with my jewelry box and my stuffed animals. Hot tears slid down my cheeks.

"Jas?" Mama called from the doorway of my room.

I wiped my eyes on one of Boo's satin corners and stuffed him into the backpack. Mama came over and pulled me into a hug.

"I know you don't want to move, honey," she said. "I don't, either. But the judge said we have to sell the house, so Daddy and I have to find new places to live."

"But why do we have to go to Aunt Carol's?" I asked, sniffing.

Mama sighed, and I knew she was trying not to get mad. "Honey, right now we just don't have enough money to get a place of our own."

"Can't we borrow some?"

"No, but as long as we're living with Aunt Carol, we can save some. Before you know it, we'll have enough to move into our own house and start our new life. You just have to be patient," Mama told me.

"I don't *want* a new life. I want my *regular* life, where I walk to kindergarten with Rosa every day." I knew I was whining, but I didn't care.

Mama sighed again, "Jasmine, we've already been over this. I'll drop you off at kindergarten every morning on my way to work."

"But Aunt Carol's house is so far away," I complained.

Mama closed my suitcase. "I'll take this downstairs," she said. "The moving van will be here any minute. Why don't you check to make sure you have everything?" She stopped in the doorway and looked around the room, then at me. "It'll be all right, Jas. You'll see."

After I was sure she'd gone downstairs, I reached into my backpack and pulled Boo out again. Until I was four, Boo'd gone everywhere with me—on family vacations, to ballet classes, even the to grocery store—and by now, he looked pretty worn out.

When I started preschool, Mama said I was too old to drag a blanket everywhere. So I stopped taking Boo out of the house. But I still slept with him every night. And when Mama and Daddy's fights got too loud, I'd wrap him around my shoulders and rub his worn blue flannel against my cheek. If I had to leave, Boo was coming with me.

I grabbed my backpack and sat down on the floor of my closet. Rubbing Boo against my cheek, I looked up at the shelves over my bed. That's where my stuffed animals had stood watch every night, keeping me safe from spooky monsters and scary shadows. Next to my bed, my ballerina clock was blinking. Mama must have unplugged it so we could put it in a box, too.

I looked above me at the empty rods where all my clothes had hung and wondered where I would put my clothes at Aunt Carol's. I pulled Boo tight around my shoulders, then stood up and began checking closet shelves and drawers. Mama had said our furniture was going into storage, and I didn't want any of my treasures going with it.

"Jasmine!" Mama called from downstairs. "The moving van's here."

I bit my lip. Mama was tired of my tears, and I didn't want to make her angry. I picked up my ballerina clock and slipped it into my backpack, then folded Boo and laid him gently on top of it. I looked around the room one more time, trying my hardest not to cry.

"Goodbye, room," I whispered. ***"Goodbye, old life."***

Postcards And Phone Calls

(Unhappy Relationship With A Stepparent)

SUMMARY:

The worse things get at home, the more Sam misses his father. Now that he's seven, Sam's hoping his mother will think he's old enough to spend the summer on the road with his dad, who's a truck driver. When a late-night argument leads to Sam overhearing something that hurts him deeply, he calls his father and pleads with him to come get him.

POST-STORY DISCUSSION QUESTIONS:

Some of the following questions can be answered with a "yes" or "no." In these cases, the child giving an answer should explain his/her reasons.

1. Sam says, "Fathers shouldn't live away from their kids." Do you agree?
2. Why does Holly suddenly start singing really loudly to the babies? What would you do if you were Holly?
3. Why does Carl give Holly all of the spaghetti? Do you think that's fair?
4. After Sam's mom talks with his dad on the phone, she's crying. Why might she be crying?
5. Have you ever been so excited you couldn't fall asleep? If so, tell about it.
6. Sam's dad says his mom didn't really mean it when she said she loved Carl more than Sam. Do you think he's right?
7. What would you do if you were Sam? His mom? His dad, Frank?

FOLLOW-UP ACTIVITY:

Materials Needed:

- ☐ Blank postcard or 3" X 5" index card and crayons or markers for each child

Distribute the postcard or index card and crayons or markers to each child. Tell the children to write a message or draw a picture they would like to send to one of their parents. Tell the children how much time they have to complete the activity. When the allotted time has elapsed, have the children share their work. Children who wish to may send the postcard to a parent.

Postcards And Phone Calls

"Sam!" Carl yells. "Get this stupid mutt out of here!"

I run into the living room. Carl's swatting Cocoa with a rolled-up newspaper.

"Come on, Cocoa!" I call. "Let's go outside."

"Worthless mutt," Carl mutters.

"You're not worthless, Cocoa," I whisper. "In fact, you're the best one in this house."

I give her a hug, fasten the leash to her collar, and yell that we're going for a walk. Not that anyone cares.

I miss my dad. His name's Frank, and he drives a truck. I think he's in Louisiana today. He's lucky. He gets to go to lots of places that are far away from people who are mean. He always sends me postcards from his trips, and I get to see him when he's home. But it's not the same as having him here all the time.

Cocoa and Mom and I moved in with Carl five years and eleven days ago, right before my half sister, Holly, was born. I was only two then. Now that I'm seven, I hope Mom will let me spend the summer with my dad.

"Maybe you can come, too, Cocoa," I say, scratching her ears. "Then we can both get away from here."

Cocoa and I run to the park and stay there for a long time. When we get home, Holly's in the back yard. Her dolls are all set up on the hammock and she's feeding them and changing their diapers.

Cocoa sniffs the dolls, then licks one of them. Holly giggles. "Cocoa!" she says.

I laugh, too, then we play house for a while. I'm the dad and Holly's the mom. We never yell at each other, and we're always gentle with the babies. I pretend I'm a truck driver. Only all of my runs are local, so I get to come home every night. Fathers shouldn't live away from their kids.

Mom gets home late and starts making dinner right away. The kitchen window's open, and I can hear Carl yelling at Mom while she's cooking. It's something about her job being more important than him. Then Holly starts singing really loudly to the babies, so I can't hear any more. I can smell the tomato sauce, though. And by the time Mom calls us for dinner, I'm bouncing up and down. Spaghetti's my favorite.

At dinner, Mom starts to put a big pile of spaghetti on my plate, but Carl stops her.

"That's enough, Alice," Carl orders. "He doesn't need all that food."

I don't argue, because I know Mom will give me seconds if I'm still hungry. Only I don't get seconds tonight, because Holly spills her first plate of spaghetti, so Carl gives her more while Mom cleans it up. He doesn't have to give her everything that's left in the bowl, but he does, even though we both know Holly won't eat it all.

Right after dinner, the phone rings. Mom grabs it, and I can tell she's talking with my dad. I bounce around the kitchen, waiting for my turn. She stays on for a long time, though, and when she hands me the phone, she's crying. I want to know why, but I'm afraid to ask.

When I get on the phone, my dad and I talk about school. I tell him I haven't gotten into trouble in a whole week, and he says he's proud of me. Then he tells me he's leaving for Tennessee in the morning, but he'll be home on Friday and he wants to see me this weekend.

When I go to bed, I'm so excited about seeing my dad, I can't fall asleep. I'm still awake when Mom and Carl go into their room. I hear them talking, but I can't make out the words at first. Then they start to get loud, and I can tell that Mom's upset.

"I just know Frank wants to take Sam away from us," Mom says, her voice sounding kind of shaky.

"So what?" Carl growls. "That's one less mouth to feed. Two if you count the mutt."

Mom starts to cry. "Carl, that's mean. I love Sam. I want him here with me."

Carl snorts, "He ain't goin' nowhere. Who else would want him?"

I put the pillow over my head, and I don't hear them for a while. Then Carl starts swearing and screaming at my mom that she loves me better than him. He's so loud, I can hear him through the pillow.

"I love you both," Mom says over and over, but Carl keeps yelling at her and making her cry until she finally says she loves him better.

I always kind of thought she did, but I never heard her say it before.

When Carl starts snoring, I tiptoe across the hall to make sure Mom's asleep, too. Then I go down to the kitchen and call my dad on his cell phone.

I wake him up, so I have to tell him the story twice before he understands me.

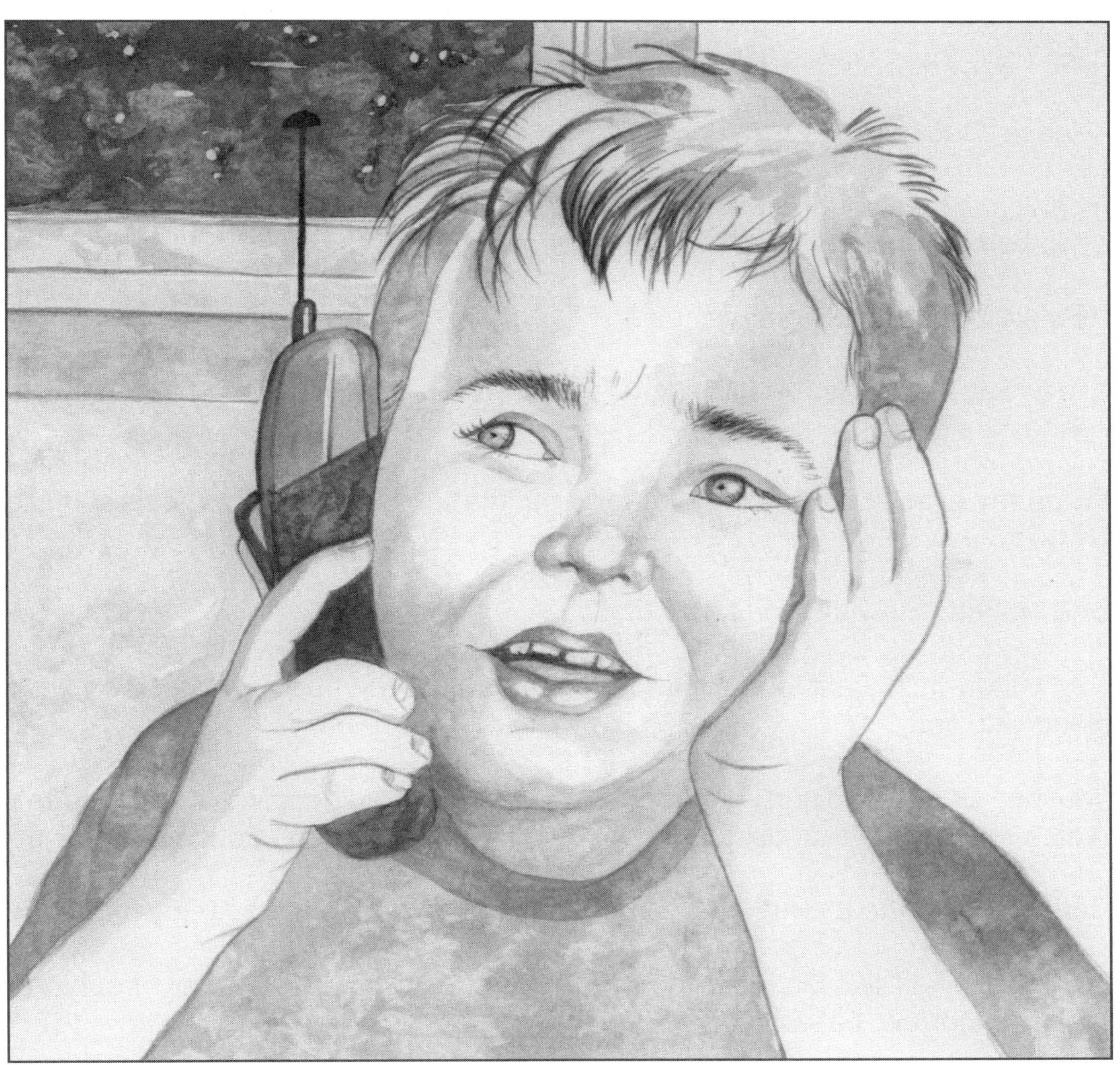

"Sam, you know she didn't mean it," Dad says. "Carl pushed her into saying what he wanted to hear."

"Can I go to Tennessee with you, Dad? Please?"

"Sammy, I'm 300 miles away! I can't exactly come and pick you up. Besides, you know you can't miss school."

"Can I stay with you when you get back? Mom won't mind. It'll be one less mouth to feed."

"Don't say that," Dad tells me. "You know that's not how your mom feels."

"Please, Dad, please?" I'm crying now. "I don't want to stay here."

"I can't just take you, buddy," Dad tries to explain. "Your mom's never agreed to a trip before, and I doubt that anything's changed."

He's wrong. Everything's changed.

"Hey, Sam," Dad says. "Do you want any special kind of postcard from Tennessee?"

I wipe my eyes and think about it for a minute. "Isn't that where the Grand Ole Opry is?" I ask.

Dad laughs. "How did you know that?"

"I saw it on TV. I want to see it for real one day. Maybe this summer when I ride along with you."

"Maybe," Dad says. Then he gets quiet again. "I've got to get some sleep, Sammy. Watch the mail for that postcard. I love you. See you when I get back."

Dad hangs up the phone. Then I hang up, too, and creep back to my bedroom.

My insides feel like oatmeal, and I just know I'm going to get into trouble at school tomorrow. I always do when I feel like this.

Cinnamon Toast And Tears

(Concern Over Whether Fighting Will Lead To A Divorce)

SUMMARY:

When Christy wakes up in the guest bedroom at Nana's for the second time in a week, she knows something's wrong. Fearful her parents will get a divorce, Christy asks Nana a lot of questions, but is still left wondering what will happen to her family.

POST-STORY DISCUSSION QUESTIONS:

Some of the following questions can be answered with a "yes" or "no." In these cases, the child giving an answer should explain his/her reasons.

1. When Christy asked her mom if she wanted to talk with her dad, why didn't her mom answer the question? Why didn't Christy ask her again?
2. How do you think Christy felt during her parents' fight? How do you think she felt afterward, when her mom grabbed some things and they went to Nana's?
3. Do you think it's normal for parents to argue? Are there any kinds of arguments it is not all right to have?
4. Why does Nana tell Christy's mother that she "can't understand why you'd want to go back to that man"?
5. Why do you think Christy feels safe in Nana's kitchen? Where do *you* go when you want to feel safe?
6. Why does Christy suddenly feel sad again when she's helping Nana clear the table?
7. Is it possible for parents to work things out after a big argument? Do you think Christy's parents will work things out?

FOLLOW-UP ACTIVITY:

Materials Needed:

- ☐ Chalkboard and chalk for the leader
- ☐ Several colors of PlayDoh® or modeling clay, child-sized measuring cups, measuring spoons, plastic or paper plates, and plastic knives for each child

Tell the children that in the story, Nana used special ingredients to make Christy's favorite French toast. Then ask them to tell what ingredients would be used to create a happy family. If necessary, suggest *love, kindness, cooperation,* etc. Write the ingredients on the chalkboard. Then ask each child to make his/her own "Happy Family Recipe" by deciding how much of each ingredient should be "served" on his/her plate. Distribute the PlayDoh or modeling clay and a plastic or paper plate to each child. Tell the children to use the measuring utensils and create their "dish" by forming the PlayDoh/clay into any shape they choose. Tell the children how much time they have to complete the activity. When the allotted time has elapsed, have the children share their finished creations.

For Younger Children: Tell the children that in the story, Nana used special ingredients to make Christy's favorite French toast. Distribute the PlayDoh and have each child create a meal for someone he/she loves. Then have the children share their creations.

Cinnamon Toast And Tears

I stretched out in bed, inhaling the spicy aroma of cinnamon French toast. Opening my eyes, I looked around. Flowery wallpaper, heavy dark furniture, blinds tightly drawn. I was in the guest bedroom at Nana's house for the second time this week. Suddenly I wasn't hungry any more.

I rolled over onto my side and tried to see through the blinds to the world outside. I wondered what my daddy was doing.

"Good morning, Christy," Mom called softly from the doorway. Her voice was scratchy. When she bent down to kiss me, I could see the dark circles under her eyes.

"Morning. Is it time to get up?" I asked.

"I'm afraid so," Mom said. "Are you okay?"

I shrugged, "Did you talk with Daddy?"

"No, not yet," Mom said.

"Do you want to?"

Mom cleared her throat. "There are some clean clothes in the closet. I'll drop you off at school on my way to work."

Mom went downstairs. While I got dressed, I tried to practice my spelling words. But all I could think about was last night's fight. It had been awful. Daddy had yelled bad words at Mom and Mom had cried a lot. Finally, Mom grabbed me and some clothes and we came here. Again.

I took a deep breath and started downstairs. Halfway down, I stopped. Mom and Nana were in the dining room, talking.

"But everything we own is there," Mom said.

"So go get it while he's at work one day," Nana replied. "I can't understand why you'd want to go back to that man."

“Good morning,” I called, walking into the dining room.

“Good morning, darling,” Nana said, trying to sound cheerful. “How did you sleep?”

I hugged Nana. She always worried about how I slept and what I ate.

“Fine, thanks,” I answered. “Breakfast smells good.”

“Let me fix you a plate,” Nana offered. She went into the kitchen and filled my plate with the cinnamon French toast I had smelled from upstairs.

When I sat down, Mom was already was at the table. She picked at her food, but I ate every bite of mine. Being in Nana’s kitchen always made me feel hungry. And safe.

After breakfast, Mom took a shower and I helped Nana clear the table. Suddenly I felt sad again.

“Nana?” I asked. “Are Mom and Daddy getting a divorce?”

Nana almost dropped the glass she was holding. “I don’t know, sweetheart.”

“Do you want them to?”

Nana tightened her lips into a line, and the wrinkles around her mouth stood out. “I want whatever makes your mother happy.”

“But what about Daddy?”

“Your daddy isn’t my child, honey,” Nana said. “Your mom is *my* baby, so I worry about her first.”

“If they get divorced, will we live here?” I asked.

Nana shrugged. “I don’t know that, either. Your mom and dad have a lot of things to talk about.”

“They don’t talk very well. Every time they try to talk, they end up yelling at each other.” I paused. “If we live here, will I ever get to see my daddy?”

Nana pulled me into a hug. “You’re just full of big questions this morning, aren’t you? I wish I had big answers for you.” Nana leaned back and looked down at me. “I think you’re going to have to ask your mother these things.”

Just then, Mom came into the kitchen. “Ask me what?”

“Nothing,” I said, pulling away from Nana and giving Mom a quick hug. “I’ll go get my backpack.”

“She’s worried,” I heard Nana say as I went upstairs.

Mom sighed. “I know. I just don’t know what to tell her yet.”

I walked upstairs slowly, wondering what would happen after school. Would we go home? Would Mom and Daddy fix things? Would we ever all live together again?

I Tried As Hard As I Could

(Unhappiness Over Dad's Choice Of A Girlfriend)

SUMMARY:

Since Daniel's parents' divorce, his father has dated a lot of women. Daniel likes some of them. He doesn't like others. But he doesn't say much, since he only sees his dad on weekends. When his dad gets involved with someone Daniel knows, Daniel realizes how little influence he has over his father's choice of a girlfriend.

POST-STORY DISCUSSION QUESTIONS:

Some of the following questions can be answered with a "yes" or "no." In these cases, the child giving an answer should explain his/her reasons.

1. Was it Daniel's fault that his father's girlfriends left him? Was it his job to be well-behaved so they would stay?
2. Can being hit by a two-year-old child really hurt? What would you have done if you were Daniel? What would you have done if you were Daniel's dad?
3. Why do you think Daniel didn't like seeing his dad "that close to Valerie"? If you were Daniel, what would you have done?
4. Why did Daniel say he didn't figure Valerie would stick around very long?
5. What does Daniel mean when he asks himself why Valerie had to be the one to stay? Should kids get to decide whom their parents date?

FOLLOW-UP ACTIVITY:

Materials Needed:

- ☐ Chalkboard and chalk, white board and markers, or poster paper and markers for the leader
- ☐ Drawing paper and markers for each child

Draw two columns on the board/poster paper. Label one "Things Kids Are In Charge Of" and the other "Things Adults Are In Charge Of." Ask the children to name things that would fit in each column, then write their responses in the appropriate column. For example, the "Things Kids Are In Charge Of" column could include *cleaning their rooms; choosing their breakfast, lunch, or clothing;* or *choosing their friends*. The "Things Adults Are In Charge Of" column could include *choosing whom they marry, taking care of the family, paying the bills,* or *keeping kids safe*.

Distribute drawing paper and markers to each child. Ask the children to draw something they wish they were in charge of. Tell the children how much time they have to complete the activity. When the allotted time has elapsed, have the children share their pictures. As each picture is presented, discuss what aspects of the wish are realistic and what aspects are unrealistic. If the wish is realistic, discuss ways to make it come true. If it is not, discuss why it is unrealistic.

I Tried As Hard As I Could

A long time ago, when I was three, my parents fought a lot. My big brother, Dustin, would take me outside and we'd ride around the block on his bike. By the time we got back, it was quiet and we could go inside.

When I was six, Dustin went to college and my parents got divorced. My mom; my dog, Snowflake; and I stayed in our house. My dad moved into an apartment near my school.

At first, it was just us guys—me and my dad—on the weekends. Then my dad met a lady named Jessica. She had two kids—Mark and Crystal. Mark was mean, but Crystal and I both liked riding bikes and playing basketball. We had a lot of fun on the weekends they visited.

Then one weekend I went to my dad's and Jessica wasn't there. The next time I went, a lady named Shirley was there. She didn't have any kids and she didn't like me very much. I heard her tell my dad I was too noisy and wild. I tried to be really quiet, but Shirley left anyway.

"It's not your fault, Daniel," Dad said. "You tried as hard as you could."

I wondered if she'd have stayed if I'd tried harder.

It went back to being just Dad and me again for a while. Then Dad met Brenda. Brenda had a daughter named Maggie who hit me all the time. She was only two, but it still hurt when she hit me.

Brenda just laughed and thought Maggie was cute.

"She doesn't mean it, Daniel," Dad said.

But I thought she *did* mean it. And it wasn't cute. I wasn't sorry when Brenda and Maggie left. I didn't try hard to keep them there.

Last year at my school's skating party, Dad spent the whole time in the snack bar with Valerie. Valerie was my mom's best friend and she was getting divorced, too. Valerie cried, and my dad patted her hand. Then Valerie cried some more, and my dad put his arm around her. Then she cried a lot, and my dad hugged her. I didn't like seeing my dad that close to Valerie, especially in front of my friends. Valerie's daughter, Ashley, didn't like it much, either.

"He's not my dad," Ashley said, punching me in the arm. "He shouldn't be hugging her."

I rubbed my arm. I wanted to punch her back, but I'm not allowed to hit girls. "I don't like it, either," I said. "So quit punching me, or I'll hit you back. Even if you are a girl!"

Valerie moved in with Dad, even though Ashley and I didn't like it. They said they were the grown-ups, so they got to decide. I really didn't like that, but I didn't figure Valerie would stick around very long.

Then one day at school, Ashley grabbed my arm as I got off the bus. Her eyes were red. So was her nose.

"They're buying a house!" Ashley cried. "My mom says they might get married."

"That's not true!" I yelled. "You're making that up!"

Ashley shook her head. "No, I'm not. I heard them talking this morning."

"But they can't get married," I said. "You already have a dad, and I already have a mom."

"Well, duh," Ashley said, as if I were the dumbest kid in the universe. "If they get married, you'll have a stepmom and I'll have a stepdad. And you'll be my stepbrother." Ashley started to cry again.

I tried as hard as I could. But as soon as Ashley couldn't see me any more, I cried, too. Why did Valerie have to be the one to stay?

Family Portrait

(Holiday Photo Session With A Blended Family)

SUMMARY:

When Becky's family goes to have a picture taken, her little brother, Teddy, is not happy. Their mama is due to have a baby soon, and Teddy's feeling a little left out. He's too young to remember other holidays, but Becky's not. During the photo session, she thinks back on other years, and realizes how lucky her family is now.

POST-STORY DISCUSSION QUESTIONS:

Some of the following questions can be answered with a "yes" or "no." In these cases, the child giving an answer should explain his/her reasons.

1. Why is Teddy so unhappy?
2. Do you think Becky and Teddy miss their "real" dad?
3. Do you think Becky and Teddy are excited about the baby?
4. Becky's mama says, "Any man can be a father, but it takes somebody special to be a daddy." What does that mean? Do you think she's right?
5. When Mama says that Greg is Becky's "real" dad for all intents and purposes, Becky decides she means that if he's her "real" daddy in her heart, he's her real daddy in her life. Do you agree? Can a stepparent ever feel like a "real" parent?
6. At the end of the story, Becky thinks, "I just know this year's holidays will be worth celebrating." Why do you think she feels that way?

FOLLOW-UP ACTIVITY:

Materials Needed:

- ☐ Plastic mugs with paper inserts that can be colored and crayons or markers for each child or
- ☐ $8^{1}/_{2}$" x 11" piece of construction paper, manila folder, glue, and crayons or markers for each child

Using crayons or markers and construction paper or the blank side of the mug insert, have each child draw a family portrait. If you are using the mug inserts, be sure to mark the overlap on the insert *before* starting to draw so that no family members are eliminated from the picture. Place the finished insert into the mug. If using construction paper, glue the finished drawing onto the inside of the manila folder. Have each child label the folder, "My Family Portrait."

Children should be encouraged to include any and all important family members and pets, not just those who live with them. Mugs or construction paper portraits may be sent home as holiday gifts.

Family Portrait

"But I don't wanna get my picture taken!" Teddy complained.

"Hush up, Teddy," I said, pushing my little brother down the aisle of the department store. "You don't want to look all messy for our family portrait, do you?"

"I don't care," Teddy said, sticking his thumb in his mouth and pulling at his tie. "I'm hot."

I was hot, too, and my red velvet dress was itchy. The store was all decorated with colorful lights and snowmen, but it wasn't even November yet. Mama wanted us to get our picture taken early, though, before the studio was full of families in holiday clothes.

Teddy was too young to remember other holidays. The Thanksgiving when Mama had made the portrait appointment and Daddy had been too drunk to show up. Or the December when Mama's eye was black and blue and she had to cancel the appointment. Then there was the year Mama had cried because we couldn't afford to have our picture taken. That was before she married Greg. Before we were happy.

"Mama's been waiting for this for a long time, Teddy, and you're not going to mess it up," I said. I pulled his thumb out of his mouth and straightened his tie. "Besides," I told him, "it won't take long. Then we can get popcorn and lemonade like Greg promised."

"I want Mama!" Teddy whined.

"She's in the bathroom," I told him.

"Actually, I'm right here," Mama said, coming up behind us and smiling.

Teddy looked at Mama's stomach. "Does the baby have to be in the picture?" he asked.

"Yes, honey," Mama told him. "The baby goes everywhere I go."

Teddy stuck out his lower lip, then put his thumb back in his mouth. He looked like he wanted to be the only baby in this family.

Greg came over to us. “Everybody ready?” he asked. “The photographer’s waiting.”

When we got inside the room where they take the pictures, Teddy cried because he couldn’t sit on Mama’s lap. Truth is, Mama doesn’t have much of a lap these days. The baby’s due next month, which is another reason Mama wanted this picture taken early. Soon, Teddy and I won’t be her only kids any more, and Mama wanted a picture with just the four of us. Well, sort of. Like she said, the baby goes everywhere she goes.

The photographer was really good. She even got Teddy to smile. I posed like she told me to and thought about presents and making holiday cookies and being a big sister again. Every once in a while, I’d wonder what my “real” father was doing.

We hadn't seen him for two years, since I was six and Teddy was barely a year old. We'd gone to Grandma's, but Mama wouldn't leave us there because she was afraid Dad would get drunk and wouldn't watch us. When he saw Mama, he got furious and they got into a loud fight. Teddy started to cry, and Mama took us both home and promised us we'd never have to do that again. Two weeks later, she met Greg. Not long after that, we became a family.

Mama says any man can be a father but it takes somebody special to be a daddy. I think she's right. Greg takes us places and plays with us and never even drinks except for wine with dinner. When I tell Mama I wish he was my "real" daddy, she tells me that for all intents and purposes, he *is* my "real" daddy. I don't know what that means, but I think it means that if he's my "real" daddy in my heart, he's my "real" daddy in my life, too.

When we finish the pictures, Greg takes Teddy out into the mall for popcorn and lemonade. Mama and I stay at the picture place to look at their stuff and pay for our pictures. While Mama's deciding on a picture frame, I look at the coffee mugs. I grab one and run over to her.

"Mama, can we get this for Greg's present?"

She looks at the mug. It says, "World's Best Dad" on it, and it has a place for a picture. Mama looks at the girl who's taking our order.

"Is it too late for us to put the photo of the kids on this one?" Mama asks.

The girl shakes her head and smiles at me. "Is that for your dad?"

I nod. "My 'real' dad. For all intents and purposes. Right, Mama?"

Mama gets all teary and I don't know if she's going to laugh or cry. "Right, Becky," she says.

Then she gives me a hug, and I just know this year's holidays will be worth celebrating.

Night Tears

(Helpless Feelings Over Parental Sadness)

SUMMARY:

Ever since Tessa's dad left, Tessa and her mom have been very sad. Tessa still catches her mom crying sometimes, and she isn't sure what to do. Even though she finds ways to manage her own feelings, Tessa still misses her dad and her old life.

POST-STORY DISCUSSION QUESTIONS:

Some of the following questions can be answered with a "yes" or "no." In these cases, the child giving an answer should explain his/her reasons.

1. What do you do when someone you love is sad?
2. Tessa's mom is pretending to be okay when she really feels sad. Why do you think she's doing this? Do you think what she's doing is a good idea?
3. Have you ever been sad because you missed one of your parents? Tell about that time.
4. If a parent gets remarried and starts a new family, what happens to his or her old family?
5. Why do you think Tessa's stepsisters "climb up on chairs and get their crayons and pretend they're doing work, too" while Tessa is doing her homework?
6. Do you think it's a good idea for Tessa to keep her feelings to herself? Whom could she tell?

FOLLOW-UP ACTIVITY:

Materials Needed:

- ☐ Posterboard with raindrops drawn on it and an umbrella for the leader
- ☐ Umbrellas with several sections cut from construction paper and markers or crayons for each child

Show the posterboard to the children. Then ask them to think of something that makes them cry. Write each answer on a raindrop. Distribute a paper umbrella and crayons or markers to each child. Show the umbrella to the children, pointing out its sections. Explain that the sections on the umbrella are like the sections on their construction-paper umbrellas. Tell them to write something that makes them feel better when they are sad on each section of their construction-paper umbrella. After they have finished their umbrellas, have them share them with the group.

Night Tears

My mommy cries a lot. She's okay during the day, but at night I sometimes hear her sobbing when she thinks I'm asleep. One night I went into her bedroom to make sure she was all right.

"I'm fine, Tessa," Mom said, pretending she wasn't crying. "Go back to bed."

So I gave her a kiss and a hug and said *good night.* I acted like I believed her, but I hugged her extra hard before I went back to bed. Sometimes people need gigantic hugs when they cry.

When Daddy first left, Mommy cried all the time. Grammy and Aunt Jan would come get me and take me shopping at the dollar store and let me buy anything I wanted. They asked Mommy if she wanted to come, but she'd just sniffle and shake her head.

"I'll be fine, Tessa," she'd say. "I'll see you when you get home."

I'm sad, too. I miss Daddy, but I try to smile so Mommy won't cry. Daddy has a new family now, with a new wife and two little girls who make noise and want to play when I'm trying to do my homework.

"Let Tessa do her schoolwork in peace," Daddy tells them, but they climb up on chairs and get their crayons and pretend they're doing work, too. They usually end up eating the crayons, though, so my stepmom takes them into the living room to play.

I wish my mommy and daddy weren't divorced. I don't like going to visit my daddy instead of having him at my house to tuck me in at night. I don't want to share him. I hate turning in homework with purple crayon marks all over it. And I don't want my mommy to cry any more.

Sometimes when I'm in bed at night, I remember how it used to be. I pretend Daddy is across the hall with Mommy, instead of across town with his new wife. I pretend he's singing to me, and when I close my eyes, I can almost hear his voice. I brush back my bangs from my forehead like he used to, and if I cry, I make sure I'm quiet so Mommy won't hear me. She's already sad and I don't want her to know that I'm sad, too. My pillow gets wet, and I turn it over and try to think about happy things like playdates and birthday parties and when I saw Mickey Mouse at Disney World. And I think that in the morning, I'll draw a happy picture for Mommy. She'll smile, and we'll both feel happy instead of sad. At least for a little while.

But it won't bring Daddy home again.

Diverse Divorce Stories For Older Children

When Irish Eyes Aren't Smiling

(Introducing The Concept Of Group Counseling For Children Of Divorce)

SUMMARY:

Erin seeks help from her guidance counselor because her parents argue a lot. When she goes to a group meeting, her twin sister, Shannon, gets angry with her for violating the family's privacy.

POST-STORY DISCUSSION QUESTIONS:

Some of the following questions can be answered with a "yes" or "no." In these cases, the child giving an answer should explain his/her reasons.

1. Shannon doesn't want everyone at school to know her parents argue. Do you think most married couples argue? Are arguments bad?
2. Amy was surprised that there were other kids who don't see their fathers. Do you think a lot of kids have parents who are divorced?
3. Jeff thought it was better when his parents were fighting than it is now when they won't even talk with each other. Does that sound strange? Which situation do you think is better?
4. Why did Erin go to the water fountain while Amy was talking with her? Was it right for Erin to hide from her sister?
5. Erin has parents and a twin sister at home. Why would she need to talk with someone else about her feelings?
6. Erin says that going to the group made her "realize that lots of parents yell and lots of them don't stay together. But when they break up, their kids can still be normal. It doesn't have to be horrible." Do you agree or disagree with her?
7. Why do you think Shannon doesn't want to go to the group? Do you think she'll keep her promise about going to see Mrs. Kain?
8. Should everyone whose parents are divorced go to a group like this?

When Irish Eyes Aren't Smiling

"**Erin!" Eleven-year-old Shannon Collins stormed into the bedroom.** "You wore my black sweater again! Now I can't wear it to school because it's in the wash. Why don't you ever ask before you borrow my stuff?"

Erin looked at her twin. "For your information," she began, her voice quivering, "it's in the dryer. You're just like Dad. Yell first and ask questions later."

"I'm *not* like Dad!" Shannon's green eyes blazed. "And I'd rather take charge than be a doormat like Mom."

Erin opened her mouth to respond, then quickly closed it again. Their mother was standing in the doorway.

Shannon's gaze snapped to the bedroom door. "Sorry, Mom," she muttered, brushing past her mother and hurrying from the room.

"She didn't mean it," Erin offered, hoping to erase the hurt look from her mother's face. "I'd-uh-better get that sweater."

Erin found Shannon in the basement, yanking clothes from the dryer and throwing them into a laundry basket.

"What's with you?" Erin asked.

"I didn't know she was standing there," Shannon replied. "It's not like I'd hurt her on purpose."

"Well, it was mean." Erin paused, "You know, there's this group at school … "

Shannon's eyes narrowed, "What kind of group?"

"For kids whose parents are divorced," Erin answered. "Maybe we should go."

"Forget it, Erin," Shannon said. "Mom and Dad aren't divorced. Besides, I don't want everyone at school to know our parents yell at each other all the time." Shannon stopped tossing laundry and looked at her twin. "How do you know so much about this? *You're* not going, are you?"

Erin shrugged, trying to look casual. "Like you said, Mom and Dad aren't divorced. We'd better get moving," she said, heading for the door and away from Shannon's penetrating stare. "We're going to miss the bus."

At school, Erin finished copying her math assignment, then slipped the yellow pass out of her science book. She stared at it for a moment, then made herself go up and give it to her teacher. "I have to go, Mrs. Walker," she said.

"Oh, that's right," Mrs. Walker said. "Jeffrey and Amy. You guys have a meeting." Erin's stomach lurched. Of course she wouldn't be the only one from her class in the group. She should have known that. She took a deep breath and walked into the hall, a few paces behind Jeff and Amy, but still careful to move quickly when she passed Shannon's classroom.

"I'm so glad this group is starting up again," Amy said as they headed down the hall, "but I don't remember you guys going before. Did your parents just get divorced?"

"No," Jeff answered. "Mine have been divorced since I was seven, but I didn't find out about this group until last week. What's it like?"

"It's cool," Amy said. "Mrs. Kain is really nice, and everything you say is confidential. I thought I was the only one in the school who never sees her dad, but there were kids in the group last year who've never even *met* their dads! Erin," she continued, "I didn't know your parents were divorced."

"They aren't," Erin said. "They just fight all the time. Mrs. Kain said it was okay for me to come today."

"My parents used to fight a lot, too," Jeff said. "Now they won't even talk with each other. Actually, I think the fighting was better."

"You're kidding!" Erin replied. "How could fighting be better?"

"At least when they fought, they talked to each other," Jeff told her. "Now they send messages through me."

"Hi, guys," Mrs. Kain said, meeting them at the door of her office. "Please take a journal and write your answer to the question on the board. You won't have to share it with the group if you don't want to."

After everyone had finished writing in their journals, Mrs. Kain explained how the group worked. Amy was right—everything they *said* in the group had to *stay* in the group. Mrs. Kain encouraged them to talk with their parents about the topics and their feelings, but they weren't allowed to tell anyone what any of the other kids had said.

At the beginning of every meeting, they would write the answer to a question in their journals. They could share their answer or pass and they could use their journals at home, too, if they wanted.

Since it was the first meeting of the year, Mrs. Kain had them go around the table and introduce themselves. Everyone was supposed to say their name, who they lived with, and how long their parents had been divorced.

Erin found out all kinds of things. Jeff's parents had gotten divorced because his mom thought his dad worked too many hours. Amy's mom refused to talk about her divorce. Juan's parents had been divorced for four years, but his mom had just moved back to Puerto Rico last summer and Juan missed her a lot. Justin's parents were best friends now that they weren't married any more. Erin didn't say much—just that she lived with her mom, her dad, and her sister and that her parents argued a lot.

"Okay, guys," Mrs. Kain said, "this has been a great first meeting."

"But we didn't do anything except meet each other!" Juan complained.

Mrs. Kain smiled. "I know. That takes up a lot of the first meeting. Feel free to write any concerns or questions in your journals and bring them with you to the meeting next week. Until then, please remember our privacy rule. Not everyone wants their family information shared with other people. If anyone needs to see me before our meeting next week, just let me know."

"Do you really think everyone will keep quiet?" Erin asked Amy as they left the office.

"Oh, yeah. Nobody wants … Erin?" Amy turned around, and put her hands on her hips. "Nice! Leave me talking to no one in the middle of the hallway."

Erin finished her drink at the water fountain and stood up, glancing quickly at the restroom across the hall. "Sorry. What were you saying?"

"Just that nobody wants the stuff they say spread around school, so they figure the best way to protect their privacy is to respect everyone else's. Erin, are you okay? You look kind of funny."

"I'm fine," Erin replied.

She was sure Amy hadn't seen Shannon go into the bathroom across the hall. But she knew Shannon had seen them.

By the end of the day, Erin was exhausted. She hadn't left her classroom all afternoon, afraid that she'd run into her sister. She knew she'd have to deal with Shannon eventually, but she didn't want to do it at school.

The minute they got home, Shannon let loose. "You went to that group, didn't you?" she said, throwing her bookbag onto the sofa. "What did you tell them?"

Erin willed herself to stay calm. "Just that Mom and Dad fight a lot."

"That's all you talked about? Parents fighting?" Shannon asked.

"That's all I can tell you," Erin replied. "What happens in the group is private."

"Private?" Shannon yelled. "If you were worried about privacy, you wouldn't have gone to that group!"

"I went to the group because I'm tired of feeling alone and scared. I needed to talk to someone."

"You can talk to me, Erin," Shannon retorted. "I know what's going on here better than anyone."

"You don't *talk,* Shannon. You *yell.* You *accuse*. You *trash Mom.*"

"I'm mad, okay?" Shannon yelled. "I just don't get why Mom doesn't stand up to Dad. Or why Dad's so hateful to her. And why they both don't see that they're wrecking our family."

"I don't get it, either," Erin said softly. "That's why I went to this group. And it made me realize that lots of parents yell and lots of them don't stay together. But when they break up, their kids can still be normal. It doesn't have to be horrible." Erin paused. "At least not any more horrible than it already is."

Shannon looked skeptical. "You learned that from one group?" she asked.

"Yeah," Erin said. "You should try it some time."

"No way. Besides, it won't change anything."

"You're right. It won't change Mom and Dad. But it might change how you feel."

"What's in this for you?" Shannon asked. "Do you get extra credit from this counselor lady for bringing people in?"

"No." Erin took a deep breath. "But I might get my sister back."

Shannon stared at her. "What's that supposed to mean?"

"The worse things get with Mom and Dad, the worse you get. You're always in a bad mood. You yell all the time. You never want to do anything fun." Erin paused. "I hate fighting with you. And I hate seeing you like this."

Shannon looked at the floor, then at her sister. "I'm sorry, Erin. You're the one person in this family I'm *not* mad at. Most of the time, anyway."

"Then try this," Erin suggested. "Just one meeting."

"I'm not ready," Shannon told her. "Besides, I don't want to talk about this stuff with kids I see every day."

"Then how about talking with Mrs. Kain? If you don't like it, you don't have to go any more. She won't make you."

Shannon hesitated. "Mrs. Kain isn't allowed to tell anybody what we talk about either? Not even Mom and Dad?"

"Nope," Erin answered, "not unless you're in some kind of danger."

"*If* I go," Shannon said, stretching out the words, "you have to promise not to touch my black sweater for a month."

Erin's jaw dropped. "A month? How about a week?"

Shannon grinned. "Two weeks, and I'll meet with her once. But I won't tell her private stuff."

"Okay, Shannon. That's up to you."

Erin smiled, thinking of Mrs. Kain's easy manner and office full of games and stuffed animals. It was only a matter of time before she got her sister back.

Engaged Is Such An Ugly Word

(Struggling With A Parent's New Relationship)

SUMMARY:

Caroline is not adjusting well to her father's relationship with Rain, a yoga teacher who is the polar opposite of her mother. Over dinner with her father and Rain, Caroline makes her feelings abundantly clear.

POST-STORY DISCUSSION QUESTIONS:

Some of the following questions can be answered with a "yes" or "no." In these cases, the child giving an answer should explain his/her reasons.

1. Do you think Caroline's father should have told her about the engagement over the phone?
2. Was it "stupid" of Caroline to hope that her parents would get back together? Do you think most kids feel this way?
3. Do divorced parents ever get back together?
4. What do you think about Caroline's behavior in the car? At dinner? Should she have been more respectful?
5. Do you think Caroline should stay with her father and Rain for the summer?
6. Did Caroline's father really "dump" her?

Engaged Is Such An Ugly Word

Engaged. What a horrible, disgusting word. Parents weren't supposed to get engaged. At least not to other people.

Caroline sighed and looked at her math homework. At least in math one plus one always equaled two. Forever.

But life wasn't like math. Her parents couldn't even make it to her thirteenth birthday without ruining her life. When she was ten, they'd separated. Last year, the divorce had become final. And now her dad was getting married again.

He hadn't even bothered to tell her in person. Instead, he'd slipped it into Wednesday night's phone call, then had the nerve to tell her they were going out to dinner Friday night to celebrate. He said he wanted Caroline to have time to get used to the idea, but Caroline thought he was afraid she'd make a scene in the restaurant if he told her there. Caroline knew better than to disappoint her parents by behaving badly in a public place. But that didn't mean she was going to greet wifey-to-be with a hug and a smile, either.

Her name was Rain. She owned a health food store, taught yoga, and sought inner peace and the meaning of life on a moment-by-moment basis. She was the complete opposite of Caroline's mother, who was too practical to worry about the meaning of life, but who made Caroline eat broccoli for reasons of her own. Caroline was intrigued by Rain with her incense and her herbs, but she didn't like her. Especially now that Rain was ruining any chance of her parents ever getting back together.

Not that Caroline had actually expected them to reunite. She wasn't stupid. But a girl could hope.

Caroline glanced down at her book. An isosceles triangle stared back at her. Two equal sides and one short side. Maybe math was more like life than she'd realized.

"Caroline? Your dad's here," her mother called from the doorway of the sitting room.

Her mother was tall and willowy, with delicate features and dark hair swept back softly into a French knot. She smelled like roses and looked regal and poised and beautiful. Caroline had often been told that she looked just like her mother, but she was still working on the regal and poised part.

“Try not to let it get to you, sweetheart,” Mom said, smoothing Caroline’s hair. “You won’t gain anything by making a scene. Do you have your phone?”

Caroline nodded. She picked up her purse and her overnight bag and kissed her mother on the cheek. On the way to the car, she tried to muster up some enthusiasm and a new excuse for avoiding the sprouts and other plant-like foods that were bound to be part of dinner. She nearly stopped cold when she saw Rain at the wheel, but relaxed when she saw her dad in the passenger’s seat.

“Hi, Caroline,” Rain said. Her voice was lilting, like those annoying wind chimes she’d insisted on hanging on the deck when she’d moved into Daddy’s house six months ago. Even from the back seat, Caroline could see the huge diamond Daddy had slipped onto the ring finger of Rain’s left hand. Yuck.

“Hello, princess,” Daddy said, taking her suitcase and putting it into the trunk.

“Hi, Daddy,” Caroline replied, kissing him on the cheek. “Where are we going?”

He closed the trunk, then Caroline’s door, and rejoined Rain in the front seat. “I thought we’d go to the Waterfront. You can get surf and turf.”

“But they don’t have soy burgers, do they? What will Rain eat?” Caroline asked sweetly.

“I’m sure I’ll manage,” Rain said, her lilt unruffled by Caroline’s sarcasm.

“Oh, good!” Caroline said. “I wouldn’t want you to starve or anything.”

Daddy took Rain’s hand and graced her with a dazzling smile. “You know I wouldn’t let either of my girls starve.”

Rain lit up like some kind of over-eager firefly. Caroline tried not to gag.

At dinner, Caroline kept busy attacking her lobster so she could ignore the lovesick looks Daddy and Rain exchanged. They talked to her about school and tennis and all the lame subjects adults brought up when they didn’t know a child very well but wanted to hold up their end of the conversation. Caroline went along with it, answering the questions with practiced enthusiasm. As long as she kept talking with her dad, she could pretend Rain didn't exist. Caroline had eaten the cherry from her sundae and was halfway into the whipped cream when Rain spoke and sucked the sweetness out of her dessert.

"Caroline," she said. "Your father had a wonderful idea. The wedding is in early June, and we'll be moved into the new house by the middle of the month. We thought it would be fun if you came to stay with us for the summer. The house has a pool and … "

Caroline nearly dropped her spoon. The house? What house? Live with them? Was she crazy?

Caroline looked at her father, willing him to interrupt this insanity and return her to her regularly scheduled life. But he just sat in his chair, sipping cappuccino and smiling stupidly at his bride-to-be, unaware that Caroline's knees had taken on the consistency of the ice cream melting in front of her.

"I have a house," Caroline replied, a little too loudly. "And I have a mother. And we go to the club to swim in the summer." Caroline's voice was beginning to shake, and so was she. "Excuse me."

She stood up, her napkin cascading to the floor. Once inside the ladies' room, she chose a stall, locked the door, and climbed up on the seat so Rain wouldn't find her. Why would she think I'd want to live with her? First she takes my dad away from me, and now she wants to take me away from my mom? Fat chance!

The door to the restroom squeaked as it opened.

"Caroline?" Rain called.

Caroline held her breath, thankful that she'd thought of standing up on the seat. The restroom door shut with a thud, and Caroline waited a minute before peering through the crack in the stall to make sure Rain was really gone. From her perch atop the seat, she pulled the cell phone out of her purse and dialed her home number. "Mom," she whispered. "I'm at the Waterfront. Can you come and get me? I'll explain later. Yes, I know. I just don't want to deal with it *tonight*. Thanks, Mom."

Caroline pushed *end* and put the phone into her purse. She took out a brush and smoothed her bangs, then peered through the crack again to make sure Rain hadn't returned. She hopped down carefully. Her legs were steadier now, and she easily strode to one of the sinks and inspected her face in the mirror. She looked neither regal nor poised. Instead, her skin was pale, her eyes pink-rimmed. Brushing her hair with a vengeance now, she reminded herself that her mother would not allow Daddy and Rain to ruin her summer. Rain might be slow, but she'd eventually learn her place. She might become Daddy's wife, but she would never become Caroline's mother.

Caroline replaced the brush in her purse and flicked her chestnut hair over her shoulder. She took one last look in the mirror, checking her eyes, hair, and composure before walking out of the ladies' room.

And into Rain.

"Are you okay?" Rain asked.

"If you cared whether I was okay, you wouldn't be marrying my father."

"Caroline, I know this is a lot to adjust to … " Rain began.

"I'm not planning to adjust to anything." Caroline said. "If you think you can take me away from my mother, become some New Age replacement … "

"I have no intention … "

"Of taking me away from my mother. Yeah, I know the speech. Just don't forget that I already have a mother. You're my father's girlfriend, and if you marry him, you'll be his wife, not my mother, no matter how big and gaudy a ring you wear."

"Caroline, that's enough."

At the sound of her mother's voice, Caroline whirled around. Her parents stood side by side, with matching glares. Her heart quickened and warmth spread through her for a split second as she saw them standing next to each other, united in purpose. Beside each other, agreeing on something, standing firmly together.

Against her.

Caroline took a breath to steady herself and turned back to Rain. "I'm sorry," she said. Her words were measured, practiced, and not quite sincere. "I shouldn't have spoken to you that way."

"Elizabeth, perhaps it's best if Caroline goes home with you this evening," her father said to her mother. "That will give her a chance to get this out of her system."

Caroline fought the tears. They wouldn't change anything. Things had come full circle. First her father had dumped her mother. And now he had dumped *her*.

Nobody's Fault

(Discovering An Extramarital Affair)

SUMMARY:

David and Denise realize there's trouble in their mother's marriage when they discover their stepfather is cheating on her. When they confront her, they are shocked to discover that the solution isn't as simple as they thought it would be.

POST-STORY DISCUSSION QUESTIONS:

Some of the following questions can be answered with a "yes" or "no." In these cases, the child giving an answer should explain his/her reasons.

1. Was David wrong to stay on the phone when he heard someone else was on the line?
2. What does Denise mean when she says Malcolm is "cheating on" their mother?
3. Why do you think Denise said, "Malcolm's a creep. All men are." Do you think she really believes all men are creeps? Do you think she's right?
4. Denise believes she and David didn't "wreck" their mother's marriage, but David wonders if they might have. Malcolm blames them, but their mother says it has nothing to do with them. Who's right? Why?
5. Are the problems between David's mother and her husband "nobody's fault"? When people get divorced, is it usually somebody's fault?
6. Should David and Denise's mother leave Malcolm? Whose decision is this?
7. What does Denise mean when she tells her mother, "I don't want *anything* that costs you your dignity"?

Nobody's Fault

David rummaged through the basket beside the kitchen telephone until he found the slip of paper with Zach's phone number on it. He picked up the phone, then froze. Instead of a dial tone, he heard voices.

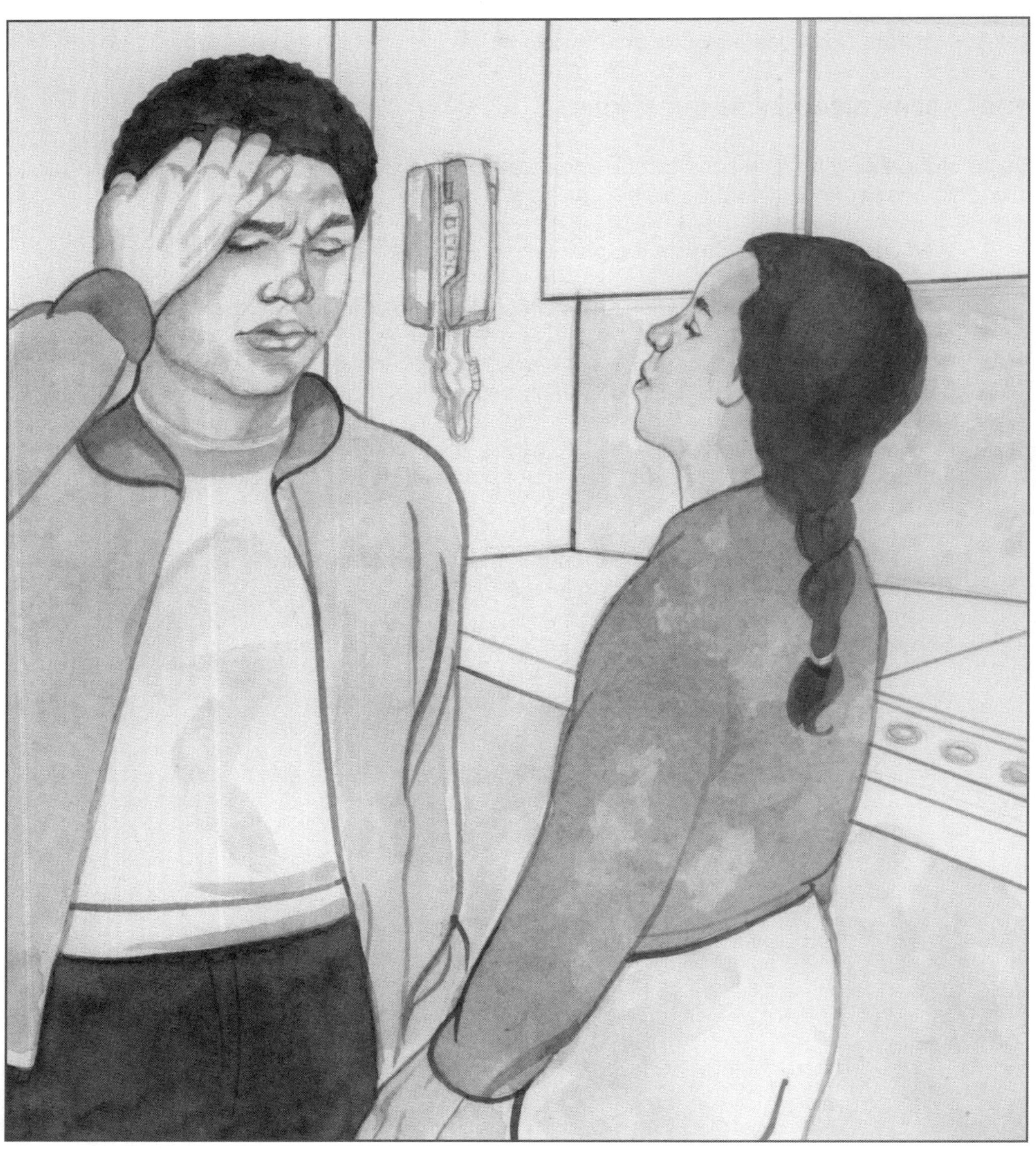

"Are you sure you'll be able to get away?" The woman's voice was soft and alluring.

"I wouldn't miss it, sweetheart," his stepfather replied. "I'll be there as soon as I can."

"I'll be counting the minutes," the woman said.

David's face felt hot and he knew he was blushing. Fighting the urge to slam down the receiver, he gently pressed the button to hang up the phone.

His sister, Denise, came into the kitchen. "Hey," she said, "you okay?"

David ran his fingers through his hair, then let his arm drop. "I just heard Malcolm on the phone … "

"Was he talking to her?" Denise interrupted.

"How'd you know?"

Malcolm Hadley strode into the kitchen, stopping abruptly. "Good morning, kids," he said. "I didn't know you were up."

Had David imagined it, or had his stepfather's eyes shifted downward when he saw them? He wanted to ask Malcolm if there was something he was ashamed of, but he knew better. "Where're you going?" he asked instead.

"Golf tournament," Malcolm answered. "Your mother's still asleep, so try to keep the noise down."

"Sure," Denise said. "We wouldn't want to wake Mom."

David walked into the living room, afraid he'd laugh if he stayed in the kitchen. Malcolm still didn't recognize the tone that Denise had spent fifteen years perfecting. Not quite sarcastic enough to be disrespectful, but nowhere near polite.

Try to keep the noise down. The words echoed in David's head. He remembered hearing that same phrase on another Saturday morning, five years earlier.

His father—his real father, not Malcolm—had been in the kitchen making pancakes when David came downstairs. Denise sat at the table, drawing a picture.

“I have a meeting with a client this morning,” Dad had said. “Try to keep the noise down while I’m away. Your mother’s still sleeping.”

“Sure, Daddy,” Denise had answered, putting the finishing touches on her picture.

“When will you be home?” David asked. “Can we play outside when you get back?”

“I’m not sure, buddy. We’ll see.”

But his father hadn’t come home. The next time David saw him was three weekends later, at his new apartment.

Mom came downstairs, and David blinked hard, trying to rid himself of the five-year-old image. Mom was dressed. Her hair and makeup were perfect, but her eyes were red-rimmed and she walked slowly, as if in a dream. Or a nightmare. She looked exactly as she’d looked the day his father had left.

“Mom, are you okay?” Denise asked.

Mom nodded, giving quick little jerks of her head as if she were trying to convince herself. Then she glanced toward the kitchen.

“He left,” David said. “Golf tournament.”

“It’s okay, Mom,” Denise said. “We know.”

Mom looked from Denise to David. “You know what?”

“That you and Malcolm are having problems,” Denise answered. “I heard you fighting last night.”

“What exactly did you hear?”

Denise touched her mother gently on the shoulder. “He’s cheating on you, isn’t he?”

Mom nodded and sank onto the sofa, tears trickling from the corners of her eyes down her cheeks.

David wanted to throw up. He looked from his mother to his sister: Denise soothing, Mom crying. He almost wondered who the grown-up was.

“Why can’t you ever pick someone who sticks around?” he blurted.

Had he really said that out loud? His mother’s silent tears became soft sobs, and David moved to hug her, clenching and unclenching his fists. “I’m sorry, Mom,” he whispered.

“It’s okay, David,” she said, standing to return his hug. “I just wish I knew the answer to your question. I’m going upstairs.”

“I’ll bring you a cup of coffee,” Denise said. She headed for the kitchen, shooting a scathing look at David over her shoulder.

David watched his mother go upstairs, then picked up the remote. He channel-surfed for a few minutes, but he couldn’t get his mother’s face out of his mind. Frustrated, he threw the remote across the room and nearly hit Denise, who was coming back down the stairs.

“Hey!” she yelled. “What’s the matter with you?”

“Three guesses.”

“Look, Malcolm’s a creep. All men are.”

“Excuse me?”

“You’re not a man yet, you’re only eleven,” Denise said quickly.

“So I’m scum because I’m a guy?”

“Let’s not go there,” Denise said as she sat down beside him. “Anyway, we’re better off without him.”

“Is he leaving?”

Denise averted her eyes. "I dunno," she said.

"You know *something!*"

Denise went over to the stairs and looked up toward their mother's bedroom.

"Is the door closed?" David whispered.

Denise nodded and gestured toward the kitchen. "He blames us," she said, once they were out of the living room.

"What? How do you know?"

"I heard them last night. He says Mom's too wrapped up in us, she doesn't have any time for him, and she never fixes herself up any more. Like she's supposed to be some 1950's TV mom!"

"You think it's true?" David asked. "You think we wrecked their marriage?"

"No, I don't think we wrecked their marriage," Denise answered loudly. "Come on, David. He knew she had kids when he met her, and it's not like we're babies or something. It's just an excuse for him to mess around with someone else."

"You're right." The voice was female, but it wasn't Denise's.

David jumped. His mother was standing in the doorway of the kitchen. Denise bit her lip and winced.

"You're right," their mother said again, putting her coffee cup on the counter. "He would have cheated on me even if I looked like Miss America every night when he came home. And make no mistake," she continued, her voice growing stronger, "this has *nothing* to do with the two of you. This is between Malcolm and me. It's not your fault."

Denise moved toward her. "Mom … "

"It's okay, Denise. I'm just sorry you overheard us." Mom turned to David. "Did you hear us, too?" she asked.

"Not you. Just him. I picked up the phone this morning and he was talking with some woman."

"Mom, what are you going to do?" Denise asked.

Her mother leaned against the counter. "I have no idea."

"We should just pack what we need and get out of here," Denise said. "We can be gone by the time he gets back."

"It's not that simple, Denise," her mother said.

"Of course it is!" Denise cried. "He's cheating on you."

"But this is our home," her mother said. "Why should *we* leave?"

Denise just shook her head. "I don't know how you can stay. I'm certainly not going to," she said, storming out of the kitchen.

Mom looked at David. "Well, we know what Denise thinks. What about you?"

"I think he's a creep, and I don't see how you can even think of staying here."

"David, think about it. I'm a receptionist at a dentist's office. He's Salesman of the Year. Why should I leave this house, move us all into some crummy apartment, and try to make ends meet on my paycheck? There are things I want for you and your sister. Things we can't afford on my salary."

"I don't want *anything* from him!"

"Really? Not your school tuition? Or a car in a few years? Or a college education?"

"Dad can help pay for those."

"David, if we move out of this house, your father's support check will cover your clothing and food. Forget private school and new bikes and video games."

"I thought this had nothing to do with us," David said. "Now it sounds like you can't afford us without him."

Denise reappeared in the doorway. “I don’t think you can afford to stay with him. How much does pride cost, Mom?”

Mom’s eyes filled with tears again. She looked from David to Denise. “Don’t you know I’d do anything for you two?”

Denise moved toward her mother. “And don’t you know there are some things you shouldn’t do for anyone?” she asked softly. “I don’t want *anything* that costs you your dignity.”

“You say that now, Denise, but when your friends are going to college … ” Mom began.

“There are other ways to get to college,” Denise said. She picked up her backpack. “I’m going to Molly’s. I’ll call you later.”

The phone rang. David reached for it as Denise stormed out the back door.

“Stop, David,” his mother said. “If it’s Malcolm, I don’t want to talk with him. Let the machine get it.”

David leaned against the counter and listened for the beep. “This is the Crown Jewel Hotel calling for Mr. Malcolm Hadley. We’ve had a cancellation, and we will be able to offer you a suite for an extended stay, after all. We can hold the suite until 6:00 this evening, and you may check in any time after 2 p.m. If you have any questions … ”

Denise came back into the kitchen. “Mom,” she said quietly, “Malcolm’s suitcase is in the garage.”

“Well,” David said, “I guess we’re staying, after all.”

It Happened Again

(The Value Of Talking Frankly About Concerns)

SUMMARY:

Diana is a mature fifth-grader who's protective of her little brother, Toby. A family outing at the park leads to a conversation that helps Diana and her mother better understand each other.

POST-STORY DISCUSSION QUESTIONS:

Some of the following questions can be answered with a "yes" or "no." In these cases, the child giving an answer should explain his/her reasons.

1. What is *child support*?

2. Why did Diana's stomach lurch when she saw her mother give Daisy's father a slip of paper?

3. What did Diana mean when she wrote, "I used to think it was just about the money, but now I think it's also about the men"?

4. Diana's mother said that she sometimes needs to be around adults. Do you think all adults feel this way? Does this mean they don't love their children?

5. Is it fair that Diana's mother gets to make all the decisions about whom she dates? Should Diana get a vote? Should Toby get a vote?

6. Should kids meet all of the people their parents date?

7. Diana's mother told her that she and her father won't get back together again. Do divorced parents ever get back together? Do you wish your parents would get back together?

8. Does divorce run in families? Why would Diana think this?

9. What did Diana's mother mean when she said, "I needed to figure out who I was before I could be somebody's wife"?

10. Is eighteen too young to get married? How old do you think you'll be when you get married? Why?

11. Is there a difference between the love parents have for each other and the love they have for their children?

12. Why did Diana hide her journal?

It Happened Again

Diana buried her head under the pillow to block out the shouting. The bed bounced. She peeked out to see her little brother, Toby, crawling toward her. He was frantically trying to scurry under her covers, his dirty yellow blanket in tow.

"Yana," he sobbed. "Make it stop."

Diana hugged Toby close and tried to relax so he wouldn't feel the tension in her body.

"It's okay, Toby. It'll be over soon."

The last word was barely out of her mouth when the apartment door slammed. Quick, muted clicks on the linoleum passed into silence as Mama's spiked heels hit the living room carpet.

Diana glanced at Toby. His thumb was in his mouth, his blanket pressed tightly against his small body. His eyes were wide open, sheer terror in shades of blue.

"It's okay," Diana whispered again. "It's over."

Toby snuggled closer and was asleep in minutes, his blond hair blending with the yellow of his blanket. Diana slid her arm from beneath his neck, then edged toward the side of the bed. It was only 5:30—way too early to go to sleep—but Toby always fell asleep after these arguments. She slipped carefully off the mattress, then pulled a small spiral notebook from beneath her bed.

"September 12," she wrote in careful purple script. "It happened again. Daddy dropped us off, and he and Mama got into a screaming fight. Mama wanted to know when he was going to pay her the $300.00 in child support he owes her." Diana paused and flipped back through the pages of her journal. August 17: $250.00. August 11: $200.00. July 27: "It happened again." July 15: "Some birthday! Is this what being twelve will be like?"

Diana looked at Toby, so peaceful now, probably dreaming about his favorite cartoon character. Was it any wonder his heroes were so huge? Somehow, she had to make the fighting stop.

Dinner that night was Chinese takeout, so Mama must have managed to get money somewhere. Toby spilled the sweet and sour sauce all over the table, and Mama screamed at him. After dinner, she apologized and took Toby into the living room to play with his trains. Diana straightened up the cramped kitchen, swept the floor, and scrubbed the rest of the sweet and sour sauce from the table. Mama had swiped at it with napkins, but Diana knew that wouldn't keep the cockroaches from feasting on it later.

The phone rang, and Diana grabbed it on the first ring. "Hello?"

"Hi, baby." Her father's voice was gentle, much softer than the last time she'd heard it. "Are you okay?"

"I'm fine, Daddy," she answered.

"How's Toby?" Dad asked

"Shook up. As usual. Daddy, why don't you just give her the money?"

Her father sighed. "Diana, if I had it, I'd give it to her. I do pay her, but it's never enough. I gave her a twenty when I left today."

So that's where the money for dinner had come from, Diana thought.

"Who's on the phone?" Mama asked.

Diana whirled, smelling the cigarette smoke before she saw her mother standing in the doorway of the kitchen.

"Thanks for the assignment, Bree," Diana said into the phone. "See you tomorrow."

Diana tried to hang up, but her mother grabbed the phone from her.

"Troy?" she yelled into the receiver. "I know it's you." She paused, and Diana heard the drone of the dial tone. "It was your father, wasn't it?" Mama said, slamming the phone down. "Apparently he has enough money for *his* phone bill."

Mama bit her lip. "I'm sorry. I'm mad at *him,* not you. Why don't you go get your shoes? We'll put Toby in the wagon and go for a walk."

Mama had changed her clothes and was on the floor tying Toby's sneakers when Diana came out of her room. Even in a T-shirt and jeans, Mama looked "dolled up," as Grandma Sandi liked to say. Her permed blonde hair was pulled up in a fuchsia scrunchee which perfectly matched the T-shirt she was wearing. The blue eye shadow, though a bit heavy, accented her eyes and made them look bluer. Diana wanted to wipe away some of the blush and lipstick, but she knew Mama would flip after having applied it so carefully. Mama worked very hard at looking too young to be the mother of a twelve-year-old. Most days, she succeeded.

"Okay, buddy, you're ready," Mama told Toby.

Toby jumped up and gave her a hug. "Thanks, Mama."

Three-year-olds forgive so quickly, Diana thought.

At the park, Diana played with Toby while Mama sat on a bench and flipped through a travel magazine. A cute guy in shorts and a T-shirt was helping his daughter swing from the hanging bars. Swing-grab, swing-grab. She couldn't quite get the rhythm, and he held her lightly by the waist, spotting her, keeping her safe. His hair was brown, like Diana's and her dad's, his manner easy and loving.

"Yana," called Toby.

Diana jumped.

"Come down the slide with me." Diana pulled her eyes away from the man and walked over the swinging bridge to the twisty slide. Toby loved the twisty slide. Diana glanced over at Mama, who was no longer looking at her magazine. She was watching the girl's father.

After a while, the girl joined Toby and Diana, and her father sat with Mama on the bench. The girl's name was Daisy. She was eight. She was visiting her dad that evening and had to go back to her mother's after they left the playground.

"Three more times down the slide, Daisy. Then it's time to go," the man called.

"Okay, Daddy," Daisy yelled.

Daisy's dad turned back to Mama, who was handing him a slip of paper. *Her phone number, no doubt,* Diana thought, her stomach lurching.

“It happened again,” Diana wrote in perfect purple script when they’d returned to the house. Toby was tucked into bed and Mama was in the shower. “We went to the park to play and Mama met a guy. She hummed all the way home and cracked jokes with Toby. She kept asking me what was wrong. I said, “nothing,” because how could I tell her in front of Toby? How could I tell her that I have a dad and I want her to get dressed up for *him,* not for some stranger on a park bench? I used to think it was just about the money, but now I think it’s also about the men.

“Writing in your journal?” Mama asked.

Diana jumped. She hadn’t heard Mama come into the room. “I was just … ”

Mama sat down on the bed. “I had one, too—a journal. Still do.”

Diana cocked her head and looked at her mother. “You have a journal?”

"Yep," replied Mama. "It helps me sort through things. I sure wouldn't want anyone to read it, though. You probably feel the same way."

Diana nodded, panic twisting her stomach, wondering if her mother wanted to read her journal.

"But if there's ever anything you want to talk about … " Mama offered.

"Are you going to go out with that guy from the playground?"

Mama laughed. "I might. But right now, he's looking for a travel agent, so I gave him my office number so he could call me about booking a business trip."

"But if he asked you on a date … "

"I'd probably go. You know, Diana, sometimes I need to be around adults."

"But you have Grandma Sandi. And your friends."

"Dates are different."

"Yeah, they're with men. And dates mean you and Dad will never get back together again."

Mama put an arm around her. "Diana, your dad and I are not getting back together."

"Because you fight so much?"

"Partly," Mama said. "But mostly because we weren't happy being married."

"Daddy was."

"Oh? Then why are we divorced?" Mama closed her eyes for a minute, then let out a puff of air. "I'm sorry. I married your dad when I was eighteen. It seemed like a good idea at the time, but I wasn't ready to settle down. We ended up disappointing each other. A lot."

"Do Toby and I disappoint you?"

"No! You do things that bug me sometimes, but I love you guys. I'm your mom forever."

"But you said you'd be Daddy's wife forever."

"You're right, I did. I don't know how to explain to you that it's different, Diana, but it is. Once you're somebody's parent, you stay their parent forever."

"Mama?" Diana asked in a quiet voice. "Will I get divorced?"

"What? Why would you ask me that?"

"Well, you're divorced. Grandma Sandi's divorced. It kind of runs in the family."

"I hope you won't make the same mistakes your Grandma Sandi and I made."

"Was Daddy a mistake?"

"No," Mama said emphatically. "But getting married at eighteen was. I needed to figure out who I was before I could be somebody's wife."

"Is that what you're doing now?" Diana asked.

"Sort of. But I know now that being your mom is an important part of who I am."

"So if we don't like something … " Diana began.

"Like hard-boiled eggs?" Mama said. "Or like me dating?"

"Both."

"Diana, some decisions you get to make, but most of them I get to make." Mama paused. "And I definitely get to make the ones that affect my life."

"But your dating affects my life, too!"

Mama paused. "I know. I'll try to remember that. But I decide whom I date and when I date. You can't be in charge of that." Her tone softened. "That wouldn't be good for either one of us."

Diana looked down at her journal and saw the words written in purple ink on the blue lines, "It happened again."

"Mama? Toby gets scared when you and Daddy yell at each other."

Mama looked sad. "I know. Do you?"

Diana pulled one shoulder slowly toward her chin and gave a half shrug. "Sort of. You never yell at anybody the way you yell at Daddy."

“That’s because no one makes me as mad as he does.” Mama thought a minute. “But I guess I could try to be quieter about it. Toby’s really scared, huh?”

Diana nodded. “He comes in here, dragging his blanket. He usually falls asleep when it’s over.”

“Your dad’s the same way. He could even fall asleep in the middle of an argument. I never understood it. You look just like him, but Toby acts more like him.”

“Is that bad?”

“No. You’re Diana, not Troy. And Toby’s Toby.” Mama looked at Diana’s bedside clock. “Time for bed,” she said.

“Okay, Mama. Good night.”

Mama leaned down and kissed her, then headed for the bedroom door. “Good night. Don’t grow up too fast, okay?”

Diana shook her head. “I won’t. Mama?”

Mama poked her head back in the doorway.

“Thanks,” Diana said.

“Sure honey. Lights out in ten minutes.”

“Okay.”

Holding her journal, Diana slid to the edge of the bed and cocked her head. When she heard the canned laugh track blaring from the television in the living room, she pushed the door closed with her foot and slid off the bed. She tiptoed across the room to her desk, then shook her head. *Too obvious,* she thought.

Looking around the room, she spied the hammock full of stuffed animals she’d ignored for years. Toby played with the platypus and the lion on the top of the pile, but he paid no attention to the plush pastel friends gathered on the bottom. Diana stuck her hand into the middle of the pile, then put her journal in the hole she’d created. Carefully arranging the animals to camouflage the book, she made sure the platypus and the lion were on top of the pile, then crept back to bed. Tomorrow she would write about her talk with Mama. But for now, the same animals that had once protected her from monsters in the closet would protect her secrets.

As Easy As Mashed Potatoes

(Financial Difficulties Force A Lifestyle Change)

SUMMARY:

Evan's mother is having trouble making ends meet since her divorce. When she goes back to work, Evan has to deal with changes in his routine as well as changes in his relationship with his best friend, who has moved on to middle school and developed new friendships.

POST-STORY DISCUSSION QUESTIONS:

Some of the following questions can be answered with a "yes" or "no." In these cases, the child giving an answer should explain his/her reasons.

1. Do you think Evan's mother has changed since the divorce?

2. If Evan and his mother need money, should Evan's father give it to them? Is it fair that Evan's mother has to go back to work?

3. How do you think Evan feels about his mother going back to work? About staying at Charlie's?

4. Why didn't Evan ask his father or grandmother for help?

5. What do you think of the way Evan handled things with Charlie and Dominic? What would you have done?

6. Evan's mother says he "looks out for her." What does that mean? Do you agree? Is that Evan's job?

7. What is *mutual happiness*? Is it always possible?

8. Why do you think Evan didn't talk with his mother sooner than he did? What would you have done?

As Easy As Mashed Potatoes

Evan rubbed his eyes and stuck his head in the doorway of the bedroom his mother used as an office. His mother's eyes were red-rimmed and a pencil stuck out of the back of her curly dark hair.

"Mom?"

She jumped. “Evan! What are you doing up?”

“I saw the light. What’s this?” he asked, picking up a paper from the pile spilling across her desk.

His mother took the paper from his hand and put it back on the desk. “Go back to bed, honey,” she said. “It’s very late.”

Evan looked at his mother’s tired face. Since the divorce, lines had seemed to pop up overnight. There’d been many days lately when he’d found her working at her desk, still unshowered and in her pajamas, instead of in her usual T-shirt, fleece pants, and sneakers. His mother had always worked at home, but she’d never been one of those moms who drove their kids to school wearing her bathrobe and bunny slippers.

“What’s wrong, Mom?” Evan asked.

His mother ran her fingers through her hair and pulled out the pencil, looking at it in surprise. “Evan, I’m going back to work,” she said. “It’s only afternoons, but that means I won’t be here when you get home from school. I’ve spoken with Charlotte, and she says she’s happy to have you stay there and hang out with Charlie until I get home.”

Charlie was Evan’s best friend, but he’d been acting weird lately. A year older than Evan, he went to middle school now, and sometimes he acted like he was too cool for his elementary school friends.

Evan looked at the papers on the desk. “We need money, don’t we, Mom?”

“Yes, honey, we do.”

“Can’t Dad help us?”

“Dad’s already paying his part, Evan.”

“When is all this going to happen?” Evan asked.

Mom hesitated. “Tomorrow. My old job at the newspaper opened up, and they need someone to fill it right away.”

"Tomorrow? Will you be here in the morning?" Evan asked.

"Yes. I'll do my freelance work after you leave for school, then go in to the paper at lunchtime." Mom paused. "Go back to bed, honey. Tomorrow's going to be a busy day."

After school the next day, Evan walked the two blocks to Charlie's house. Charlie was already there, playing a video game with Dominic, a seventh grader Evan didn't like very much. They ignored Evan, so he plopped his books on the kitchen table and gratefully accepted the snack Charlotte offered him. He was halfway through his math homework when Charlie came into the kitchen.

"Hey, Ev," he said, grabbing an apple from the counter. "Wanna skateboard?"

"Where's Dominic?" Evan asked.

"He left. Come on. Do your homework later."

By the time the boys arrived at the skate park, things felt normal again. Charlie was friendly and fun. Evan wanted to ask him why he'd been such a jerk at the house, but kept quiet because he didn't want to ruin things.

Evan's mom was waiting for him when he and Charlie got back. Driving home, she couldn't stop talking about her day. "It's so great to work with other people again," she said excitedly. "And the newsroom is just bursting with energy. How were things at Charlie's?"

"Fine," Evan answered. "I got some homework done. Can we get a pizza to celebrate your new job?"

Mom thought for a minute. "I suppose we could splurge a little."

By the end of the week, Evan had fallen into a routine. After school, he trudged to Charlie's, thinking of all the other places he wished he could go instead. He thought about calling his dad to see if he could pick him up after school. But that would just launch another round of arguments between his parents, and he definitely didn't want to deal with *that.* Grandma had just retired, and Mom wouldn't want to impose, so calling her was also out of the question. And Mom would never agree to let him stay home alone. Since the divorce, Mom had become even more protective of him. It was as if she was afraid she was going to lose him, too. This new job made her happier than Evan had seen her since before Dad left. There was no way he was going to upset her just because Charlie was a jerk for an hour a day.

So Evan went to Charlie's and sat in the kitchen with his snack and his math until Dominic or Jason or whoever finally went home. Then, when it was just the two of them, Charlie would be his old self. He and Evan would ride bikes, play video games, or skateboard and things were like they had always been.

One Friday afternoon, Evan walked into Charlotte's kitchen, listening for the shouts and video-game noises that usually came from the family room. Instead, he heard Dominic's voice. "What's the deal with that Evan kid, anyway? Why's he always hanging out in your kitchen? Doesn't he have his own house?"

"Yeah," Charlie said, "but his mom works after school, so he stays here until she gets home. It's a real pain."

Evan swallowed hard, then stalked to the doorway of the family room. "You think I *want* to be here?" he yelled. "You think you guys are such great company?"

Charlie looked at him for a moment, then dropped his gaze to the floor. Dominic just smirked.

Evan stormed across the kitchen and out the back door. He sat down hard on the porch and put his head in his hands. Charlie's voice echoed in his head. *He was a pain? Charlie should try looking in the mirror.*

Evan stood up, ready to go home, to school—anywhere but back into Charlie's house—and heard the door shut. Charlie bounded down the porch steps, holding his skateboard, never looking back.

Dominic brushed past and whispered in his ear. "See ya, Mama's boy."

Evan swung. His fist grazed Dominic's chin, and he crouched, readying himself for a response. Instead, he felt soft pressure on his shoulders.

"I think you'd better go," Charlotte told Dominic.

Dominic rubbed his chin and grabbed his skateboard. He walked slowly down the steps, still looking at Evan and Charlotte.

Once Dominic was gone, Evan pulled away and ran down the steps. He kept running, away from Charlie's, away from Dominic, away from Charlotte's voice calling out to him. He ran until he reached his own back porch, then flung his backpack up the steps.

By the time Mom got home, she had already talked with Charlotte. She knew about Dominic.

"Why didn't you tell me you were unhappy?" she asked softly, sitting down next to Evan on the steps.

Evan looked at her, unable to stop the tears. "Because *you* were happy," he said. "Besides, where else was I going to go?"

"We'd have figured something out. How long have you and Charlie been having trouble?"

Evan shrugged. "A while."

Mom sighed. "I have an idea. How would you feel about staying here with Grandma after school?"

"I thought Grandma was busy."

"Not so busy that she'd want you to be miserable," Mom said. "I don't feel comfortable asking her to come every day, though, so we'll have to make some other arrangements, too."

"Can't I stay here by myself?"

"Evan, I don't think you're ready to be here alone every day after school."

"Is it because I ran away from Charlie's?"

"No," Mom told him. "I'm not happy about what happened this afternoon, but I understand that you were upset. Still, we'll have to set some ground rules for the days you're here with Grandma after school."

"I guess ground rules are better than being grounded." Evan paused. "Once I prove I can handle the ground rules, would you maybe consider letting me stay here alone one day a week?"

Mom thought for a moment. "Honey, it takes more than just handling ground rules to convince me that you're ready to stay home alone. You'll have to prove that you're mature enough to handle the responsibilities of being here by yourself."

"Could I do some jobs or something?" Evan pleaded. "Get dinner started?"

"Evan, the stove is the last place I want you to be when you're here alone."

"I wouldn't have to use the stove. I could do other things, like setting the table or making a salad. You know, stuff like that." Evan looked at his mother's teary eyes. "I'm sorry, Mom. I didn't mean to upset you."

"You didn't," she answered. "I'm just realizing how fast you're growing up. You really do look out for me, don't you?"

"Mom, don't get all mushy on me."

Mom grinned and brushed back a tear. "Tell you what. Let's see what days Grandma is available, then go from there. You may have to go to Charlie's a couple of days a week. Think you can handle that?"

"I guess," Evan answered. "Actually, Charlie's not such a jerk when we're at the skate park. I'll just do my homework until his friends leave."

"Evan," Mom went on, "you do realize that no matter how well you do with the ground rules here, I won't believe you're responsible enough to stay home alone if you run away from Charlie's again? And no matter how happy you think I am, you need to tell me when you're unhappy. Deal?"

"Deal. It would be kind of cool if we were both happy, huh?"

Mom ruffled his hair. "It would be very cool. Come on, Mr. Independence. Let me introduce you to the fine art of peeling potatoes."

"Since I'm going to peel them, do I get to decide what we make with them?"

"I thought we were going for mutual happiness here."

"Okay, okay," Evan said. "How about mashed?"

"Just what I was thinking."

"Who knows, Mom? Maybe this mutual happiness thing will be as easy as mashed potatoes!"

Bottles, Blondes, And Peach Polyester

(Taking Care Of An Alcoholic Mother Raises The Issue Of Who Is The Parent)

SUMMARY:

Leslie is the caretaker child of an alcoholic mother. When her mother's secret threatens to become school gossip, Leslie decides that maybe her feelings are just as important as who will take care of her mother.

POST-STORY DISCUSSION QUESTIONS:

Some of the following questions can be answered with a "yes" or "no." In these cases, the child giving an answer should explain his/her reasons.

1. After Leslie says *good night* to her mother, Leslie thinks she understands why her dad left. What does she mean? Is it her mother's fault that her father left?
2. Leslie doesn't tell her mother much about the wedding, but she gives Jodi and her mother details about it. Why do you think she does this?
3. When Jodi asked Leslie about her mother's reaction to her father's remarriage, Leslie said, "She's handling it." Why doesn't she tell Jodi about her mother? Do you think Jodi knows?
4. When Mrs. Manning asked Leslie to stay for dinner, why did Leslie tell Mrs. Manning that she promised her mom she wouldn't be gone long?
5. Why didn't Leslie tell anyone that she wants to live with her dad and Julie?
6. Why is Leslie's mother so different in the morning?
7. Does Leslie want her mother to come to the presentation at school? Do you think Leslie's feelings are fair?
8. Why doesn't Leslie let her mother stay at school?
9. What do you think Leslie wants to discuss with her dad and Julie?
10. How do you think Leslie feels about her mother?

Bottles, Blondes, And Peach Polyester

They never actually yelled at each other. In fact, some days they hardly spoke at all. Leslie had learned by the time she was three that anger isn't always loud.

When Leslie was nine, she found the ring. She'd been helping her mom put laundry away when she discovered the box wedged into a corner of her dad's underwear drawer. A black velvet box, with a jewelry store's name in gold script on the lid. She had wanted to run and show it to her mother, to tell her that Daddy was going to fix everything. But even at nine, she knew better.

Instead, she waited. A month later, Daddy moved out. The next week, the ring reappeared. This time, on the left hand of a blonde named Julie. She was a blue-eyed beauty not much taller than Leslie, and she was going to be Leslie's stepmother.

Leslie shook her head to chase away the memories, then gently pushed on the door of the den. "Mom?" she called softly. "I'm home."

Leslie's mother turned. Her eyes were bleary and a sour grin twisted her lips. "How was the big event?"

"Good." Leslie plopped into the armchair. "My dress itched."

"It's no wonder, with all that ridiculous lace. How is Princess Julie?"

"Mom … " Leslie began.

"Sorry. How are your father and his new wife?" Her tone was sickeningly sweet, the words slurred.

Sober, Leslie thought. *And happy. Unlike you.* "Fine," she said instead, her eyes scanning the room. "Did you have a good weekend?"

"Just peachy." Mom giggled and lifted a glass of fruity liquid in a mock toast.

Leslie spied the empty liquor bottle on the floor under the sofa. "Do you need anything before I go to bed?" she asked.

"N-n-nope!" Mom slid into the word and nearly slid off the sofa. "Go rest up from all the festivities. Tomorrow we go back to our dull little world."

"Good night, Mom." Leslie leaned down to kiss her mother on the cheek, holding her breath to escape the sweet and sour aroma of unbrushed teeth, unwashed hair, and peach schnapps. She walked out of the den and quietly closed the door. On nights like this, she understood why her father had left.

The next morning, Leslie got ready for school while her mother slept. Before leaving, Leslie checked to make sure her mom was still breathing, then grabbed her backpack and closed the door quietly behind her. She met her best friend, Jodi, at the bus stop.

"So how was it?" Jodi asked.

"Perfect!" Leslie said. "Julie looked gorgeous, and she and Dad smiled the whole weekend."

"How's your mom?"

"She's handling it," Leslie said. "Hey, did you get the paper for the brochures? That social studies fair is tomorrow."

Jodi took the cue. "Yep. Want to work on them at my house after school?"

"Sure. I just need to get something at home first."

When Leslie got home after school, the house was empty. A piece of paper sticking out of the neck of the empty schnapps bottle told her that Mom was at work. Leslie threw the bottle into the recycling bin and the scrap of paper into the trash and left her mother a note that she was at Jodi's.

On the way over, Leslie thought about the weekend. It would be so cool if she could live with Dad and Julie! She wouldn't even have to change schools, just houses. But who would take care of Mom?

Leslie rang the doorbell at Jodi's house. Jodi's mom came to the door, dressed in an aqua silk suit she must have worn to work that day. Mrs. Manning was petite and blonde. Like Julie.

"Leslie! Come in," Jodi's mom said. "So—how was the wedding? Jodi tells me you had a good time."

Leslie grinned. "I did. I got to be the decoy for the photographer so my dad and Julie could talk with their guests. They'll have more pictures of me in their wedding album than of each other!"

"I'll bet you looked beautiful," Jodi's mom said as she brushed a blonde curl from Leslie's face.

"And guess what?" Leslie said. "I caught the bouquet!"

Jodi appeared behind her mother. “You didn’t tell me that.”

Leslie giggled. “But my dad said I can’t get married until I’m twenty-five.”

Jodi rolled her eyes. “My dad says the same thing to me. Hey, did you bring the recipes?”

“Got them right here,” Leslie said, holding them up.

“Great!” Jodi said. “Once we type them in, we’re all set to print out the brochures. We should be finished by dinner time.”

“Leslie, would you like to stay for dinner?” Jodi’s mom asked.

“No, thanks, Mrs. Manning. I promised my mom I wouldn’t be gone long.”

When Leslie got home, her mother’s car was in the driveway, but the house was dark. Leslie tiptoed into the den and found her mother sprawled across the couch. She was still dressed in her peach polyester waitress uniform. A half-empty bottle of liquor sat on the coffee table. Leslie got a blanket and covered her mother. She took the bottle into the kitchen, dumped its contents down the drain, and tossed it into the recycling bin. Then she made herself a peanut butter and jelly sandwich and ate it at the kitchen table while she finished her homework. Before she went upstairs, Leslie kissed her mother *good night.* Mom hadn’t budged since Leslie had checked on her three hours earlier, and she remained sound asleep when Leslie kissed her.

Leslie woke to the smell of coffee and bacon and the vocal stylings of Frank Sinatra. Wearing sweatpants and the T-shirt she’d slept in, she ran downstairs. Place mats and floral paper plates graced the dining room table. Her mother was in the kitchen, singing along with Frank.

“Good morning, honey,” Leslie’s mother said in a cheery voice. When Mom hugged her this time, Leslie smelled toothpaste and bath gel. “I’m sorry I crashed on you last night. Did you get dinner?”

“I had a sandwich,” Leslie answered. “What time did you go upstairs?”

“Around midnight. You were sound asleep.”

Most eleven-year-olds are sound asleep at midnight, Leslie thought. “This looks really nice,” she said aloud, gesturing to the table.

Mom grinned. “Breakfast is the most important meal of the day,” she trilled. “You can’t learn on an empty stomach.”

Or on one full of alcohol, Leslie thought. “Do you work tonight?” she asked.

Mom wrinkled her nose. “Double shift. I go in at noon. Guess I won’t make it to your presentation at school this afternoon.”

Leslie sighed, partly out of relief and partly out of disappointment. She knew Jodi’s mom would make her feel less lonely, but it wasn’t the same as having a parent of her own there. Dad and Julie were on their honeymoon, and now Mom would be working. Which might not be a bad thing, considering the bender she’d been on.

“It’s okay, Mom.”

Mom put eggs on Leslie’s plate. “You sound disappointed.”

Leslie shrugged. “I feel like an orphan sometimes when everyone else’s parents are there.”

As Mom turned to go back into the kitchen, Leslie caught a glimpse of her face. Was that a tear tracking through her blush?

“But it’s okay,” Leslie added. “Lots of kids’ parents have to work. Should I stay at Jodi’s tonight?”

Mom cleared her throat. “If it’s okay with her mom. I won’t be home till late, and I’d feel better if you weren’t here alone.”

Leslie finished her breakfast and went back upstairs to get ready for school. Frank was still crooning, and the clanging of pots and pans and the sound of running water providing a less-than-harmonious backup. But Mom had stopped singing.

Leslie's class spent the entire morning setting up for the fair. The students transformed the classroom into a travel agency, with different stations representing different regions of the country. In addition to information, each booth featured food from its region, along with recipes for preparing it. Leslie and Jodi's group had the Middle Atlantic states, so their snacks included crab dip, apple fritters, and a foot-long Philly cheese steak sliced into sections. Leslie figured they'd spend the next two days writing *thank you* notes to the PTA and the local businesses that had helped them with the food.

The parents began arriving right after lunch. Leslie was grateful for the room setup, which made it hard to tell whose parents were there and whose weren't. She kept busy straightening brochures and answering questions about her region. To make sure the parents quizzed the "travel agents," Leslie's teacher, Miss Tyler, had given each guest a list of suggested questions.

"Aren't you supposed to have beer with crab?" The husky whisper was unmistakable, and the aroma of stale schnapps was sickening.

"Mom! What are you doing here?" Leslie whispered.

"This is a fair for the parents, isn't it?"

Leslie bit her lip. Her mother's words were slurred, and her uniform looked as though she'd slept in it. "Yes, but … I thought you had to work."

"I did. I do. I just … took a break." Leslie's mom giggled, "Aren't you glad to see me?"

Leslie looked around. Amid the fathers in navy suits and the mothers in khakis and polo shirts, the bottle blonde in peach polyester stood out like a skunk at a lawn party. And smelled about as pleasant as a skunk.

"Mom, you need to go." In one long stride, Leslie came out from behind the booth and gripped her mother's arm. They were halfway to the door when Jodi and her mom came in, holding a fresh bowl of crab dip.

"Hello, Crystal," Mrs. Manning said to Leslie's mother. "What a surprise! Jodi said you couldn't come."

“My mom and I were just going for more crackers,” Leslie said. “Jodi, can you be the designated travel agent for a while?”

Without waiting for an answer, Leslie pulled her mother to the doorway of the classroom. “You can’t be here like this,” she said through clenched teeth, nudging her mother into the hallway. “I’ll call a cab.”

Leslie knew her mother was crying. She could hear the sniffles. She vaguely heard her mother’s pleas over the deafening roar of her own anger, but she was busy trying to get down the hall without making a scene. When they reached the guidance office, Leslie convinced Mrs. Keller to let her use the phone, saying that her mother’s car wouldn’t start. When the cab arrived, Leslie put her mother into it, then asked Mrs. Keller if she could use the phone one more time.

“Leslie, are you all right?” Mrs. Keller asked.

Leslie nodded. “I’m fine. I just need to leave a message for my dad.”

“Okay,” Mrs. Keller replied. “I’ll be next door if you need me.”

Leslie blinked back tears and picked up the phone. By the time she heard her father’s voice on the answering machine, she was calm again.

“Hi, Daddy. Hi, Julie. It’s me. Please call me as soon as you can. We need to talk.”

Leslie replaced the phone in its cradle, blew her nose, and headed back to class. The anger was quieter now, the crisis averted. It was time for her to be a kid again.

Scraps Of A Family

(Finding A Way To Preserve Pre-Divorce Memories)

SUMMARY:

Marci's father isn't coming for her birthday, and Marci isn't handling her disappointment well. A trip to the mall gives her an idea that might preserve her memories of her family, even if she can't reunite her parents.

POST-STORY DISCUSSION QUESTIONS:

Some of the following questions can be answered with a "yes" or "no." In these cases, the child giving an answer should explain his/her reasons.

1. When she finds out her father isn't coming, Marci thinks that birthdays stink. Do you think she really means it?
2. Why did Marci yell at her mom when it's her dad who's not coming? Have you ever yelled at someone when you were angry with someone else?
3. Do you think this is the first time Marci's dad has disappointed her? Why or why not?
4. Marci said she doesn't think her family will ever be together again. Do you think she's right?
5. Why is Marci's scrapbook so important to her? Will it solve all her problems?

Scraps Of A Family

Marci stood at the top of the stairs, trying to block out the words.

"I understand, Jack," her mother said into the telephone, "but Marci won't."

Her dad wasn't coming for her birthday. Even though he'd promised. Even though Marci had begged. Now she couldn't even *pretend* they were still a family.

Divorce stinks and so do birthdays, Marci thought, dragging herself down the stairs.

"Ready to go?" Mom asked, looking up from her shopping list.

"Was that Dad?"

Mom paused, looking at Marci's expression. "You heard. I'm sorry, honey," she said softly. "I know your birthday won't be the same without your father, but we can still have fun."

"Why didn't you *make* him come?" Marci demanded. "You never make him keep his promises. I hate this! Why can't I have a normal family like everyone else?"

Marci stomped up the stairs and grabbed the cordless phone. Her brother, Brad, barreled out of his room and ran right into her.

"Hey, watch where you're going!" Marci snapped.

"Sorry, Mars," Brad said. He waved his hand in front of her face. "You all right? You look kind of dazed."

"Dad's not coming."

"Oh," Brad said. "What made you think he would? He never does." Brad eyed the phone in Marci's hand. "You gonna use that?"

Before Marci could answer, the phone rang.

"Hello?" Marci made a face at her brother, and took the phone into her room.

"Becca!"

"Hey, Marci! Did your dad call?"

"Yeah," Marci whispered. "He's not coming."

"But you'll see him at your grandmother's, right?"

"It's not the same. I don't think my family will ever be together again."

"The whole family togetherness thing is overrated," Becca insisted. "Alex opens half my presents before I can stop him. You want a four-year-old brother?"

Marci grinned. "No thanks. Brad's all broken in."

"Hey, call me after you get back from shopping, okay? I want to hear all about it."

Marci smiled and hung up the phone. She grabbed her stuff and headed downstairs.

"Mom?" she said softly. "I'm sorry."

Her mom hugged her. "I know this is hard."

"Where's Brad?" Marci asked.

"Outside on his bike," Mom said. "Why don't you go and watch for Grandma?"

Marci wandered into the living room and plopped down on the sofa. Her parents used to sit here on birthdays, side by side, all smiles as she or Brad tore open their gifts. They'd beamed at Marci when she'd gotten the dollhouse she'd begged for and grinned at Brad when he grimaced at clothes.

But not at each other. They hadn't smiled at each other, she thought.

The doorbell rang, shattering the unwelcome image. "I'll get it!" Marci yelled, running to the front door and throwing it open.

"Hi, sweetheart," Grandma said. "Ready to shop till you drop?"

Marci hugged her and pulled her inside. "Grandma's here!" she yelled.

"And Brad's off to Jeremy's," Mom said, coming into the foyer. "Everybody ready?"

Ten minutes later, Marci slumped in the back seat of the car, listening to her mother and grandmother chatting about party favors.

"What do you want for your birthday, Marci?" Grandma asked.

My family, all together in one room with no fighting, Marci thought. "Oh, anything's fine, Grandma," she said aloud.

The mall was noisy and way too busy. Shoppers rushed in and out of stores, and lines stretched on for miles inside stores and outside restrooms. Marci followed her mother and grandmother onto the escalator bound for the second floor.

"Where do you want to go, Marci?" her mother asked.

Marci looked around. The video store was too far down the mall. Mom would never agree to that. At the top of the escalator, a store called *Super Scrapper* had a display window filled with paper, pens, and stickers. Best of all, the store was empty.

"I'll try that place," she answered, pointing to the store's display window.

"Okay," Mom said. "We'll meet you there."

Marci wandered into the store. Scrapbooks in colors ranging from white to deep purple were lined up on shelves. Rolls of stickers filled one wall and racks held stacks of paper, carefully sorted by color, size, and design. There were scissors with fancy blades and more kinds of glue than Marci had known existed. Displays held pages filled with photos of weddings, birthday parties, and holidays. Lots of pictures of smiling families. Marci's eyes filled with tears.

"May I help you?"

Marci glanced at the perky sales clerk who had appeared at her side. "I don't know," she said.

"Are you looking for a gift?" the clerk asked.

"Umm … Who made all this stuff?"

"Our instructors. We have classes to teach people how to make scrapbooks."

"Classes? Really?"

"Just to get you started and familiarize you with the products. If you've ever done a collage, you can make a scrapbook page. All of our products are guaranteed to keep your memories safe for years and years," the clerk explained.

Safe memories, Marci thought. *I like that.*

"Marci?"

Marci jumped. Her mother and grandmother were standing in the doorway.

"Thanks," Marci said quickly to the clerk.

"I know what I want for my birthday," she announced, running to her mother and grandmother. "Pictures!"

Her mother looked surprised. “Pictures?”

“Old pictures,” Marci said. “From before the divorce.”

Her mother paused. “Marci, I don’t know … ”

“It’s okay, Mom, really,” Marci said. “I want to make a scrapbook. You’ve always told me that at one time you and Dad loved each other very much. I want to see what that looked like.”

Mom turned away, blinking back tears.

“Besides,” Marci said, “this way, I can put our family back together. At least on paper.”

“I think that’s a marvelous idea, sweetheart,” Grandma chimed in, putting an arm around Marci. “I have a box filled with photographs from birthdays and holidays. That should get you started.”

Marci looked at her mother. Tears still shone in her mother’s eyes.

“I know it’s not for real, Mom,” Marci said softly, “but I want to try it.”

“I agree with your grandmother,” her mother said. “It’s a marvelous idea.”

“Could we get stuff for one page today?”

Her mother raised her eyebrows. “I thought this was supposed to be a present.”

“Well, since Dad’s not coming, I’d like to make a birthday page now. That way, I can remember my birthday the way it used to be.”

“Marci … ” her mother began.

“I know, I know. This is the way things are now.” Marci paused. “But sometimes I miss the way things were.”

“All right, just a few things,” Mom relented. “And while you’re at it, show me some things you’d like for your birthday.”

“Thanks, Mom,” Marci said, hugging her mother. “I guess there’s some hope for this birthday, after all.”

Fathers And Other Strangers

(An Absentee Father Unexpectedly Comes Into A Child's Life)

SUMMARY:

Monica lives with her mother and has never met her father. When Monica's father decides he wants to meet her, her usually calm mother becomes extremely distraught and Monica struggles to deal with a flood of feelings about a man she's never known.

POST-STORY DISCUSSION QUESTIONS:

Some of the following questions can be answered with a "yes" or "no." In these cases, the child giving an answer should explain his/her reasons.

1. Why did Monica say she doesn't have a father?

2. Monica's mother said that not knowing Monica is her father's loss. Do you think she's right?

3. Monica's mother also said that some men just aren't ready to be parents. What does she mean? Can this be true about some women, too?

4. Why is Monica afraid to meet her father?

5. Monica's mother said, "But he *is* your father, and I don't have any right to keep you away from him if he wants to see you." Do you agree? Do you think one parent should ever keep a child from seeing the other parent?

6. Monica is twelve, and is meeting her father for the first time. Why do you think he wants to meet her now? Do you think most parents who have been away that long suddenly decide they want to meet their children?

Fathers And Other Strangers

Monica heard her mother slam the telephone onto its cradle. She sat up straight in her bed and strained to listen. Silence. She tiptoed to the door of her mother's bedroom. Her usually even-tempered mother was pacing back and forth, muttering under her breath. If Monica didn't know better, she'd swear her mother was saying things that she'd ground Monica for saying.

"Mom?"

Her mother whirled around. "Monica! I thought you were in your room."

"I was. Who was on the phone?"

Her mother's olive skin became ruddy with anger. "Come," she said, patting the bed. "Sit."

Monica did as she was told. "Mom, are you all right?"

"I am angry. Very angry. That was my lawyer on the phone."

"Are you in trouble?" Monica asked.

"No." Her mother's voice was calm, but her eyes were blazing. "Monica, your father wants to meet you."

"My father?" Now *Monica's* eyes blazed. "I don't *have* a father."

"Yes, unfortunately, you do. He's not a bad person," her mother added quickly, "just an absent one."

"Why can't he *stay* absent?" Monica asked.

"I wish I knew," her mother sighed.

Monica didn't sleep that night or the next. She kept trying to picture her father in her mind, imagining how it would be to meet him, what he would look and sound like, what he would say. She was angry and resentful at first. But as the nights wore on and sleep didn't come, she began mentally asking him the questions that had tortured her for twelve years. Where had he been? Why had he left her?

Monica's mother had always told her that not knowing her was her father's loss, that some men just weren't ready to be parents. Her mother had never said that *she* hadn't been ready, but Monica couldn't imagine that she had been. Her mother had been 20, a year shy of her college graduation, when she found out she was pregnant. She had wanted to be a doctor, but medical school and babies didn't mix when there was no one else at home at night.

So Monica's mother had gone to school part-time and had become a physician's assistant. For as long as Monica could remember, her mother had stressed the importance of education and discipline.

So when Monica awoke to clouds and storms after her sleepless nights and her mother suggested she stay home from school, Monica was puzzled.

"But it's Thursday! I have art class and my flute lesson. And tomorrow's my social studies test, and my book's at school," Monica protested.

"Monica, you are exhausted."

"But you never let me stay home because I'm tired. You always say I'll get a second wind." Monica paused, "Is this about *him*?"

Her mother sighed and rubbed her temples. "I guess I'm just a little tired myself."

When Monica was ready to leave for school, her mother handed her a note. "Please be sure to give this to your teacher. I want to fill her in on what's happening."

"Did you tell her about *him*?" Monica asked.

"Yes, but I told her you'd rather not discuss it."

"Thanks, Mom." Monica hugged her mother. "I'll see you after school."

Clutching the note, Monica ran out the back door and down to the bus stop. Climbing onto the bus, she collided with Kevin Miller and the note fell to the ground. She scrambled back down the steps of the bus and retrieved the note from a puddle. The front of the envelope was soaked, the ink beginning to blur. Monica tore open the envelope, put the letter into her backpack, and hurried onto the bus.

When she got to her seat, she slid across to the window and looked out at the rain. The wet envelope was still in her hand, and she crumpled it up and put it in her coat pocket. She opened the front section of her backpack and peeked in at the note. *Maybe I should open it so the ink doesn't run,* she thought.

She reached into her backpack and pulled out the note. It was damp, but not waterlogged, and the writing inside appeared to be fine. Monica glanced around. Everyone was involved in their own conversations and flirtations. No one was paying attention to her. She held the letter in her lap. The edges of the paper were wet, and stuck slightly when she pulled them. *It's a good thing I decided to open it,* she thought.

Her mother's tiny handwriting was hard to read, but Monica was used to it. Monica squinted as she read her mother's description of the days since her father had called. She was shocked to discover that her mother hadn't slept much since the phone call, either. Monica's mother requested that Mr. Rossi hold her accountable for her work, but that he also understand that Monica was under a lot of stress and preferred not to discuss the issue.

Feeling guilty for betraying her mother, Monica was about to refold the note when the word *NOT* jumped out at her. What was Mr. Rossi NOT to do?

Monica gasped. The last paragraph of the letter reminded Mr. Rossi that there was a notation in Monica's file that she was to be released to no one except her mother, and that she was NOT, under any circumstances, to be released to her father.

Her mother was afraid her father would come to get her at school! Was she afraid he'd kidnap her? Monica hurriedly folded the note and put it back into her bookbag.

Whenever she had to leave her classroom that day, Monica made sure she wasn't alone. Erica and Jenny were in her flute ensemble, and the whole class went to the art lesson together. She made no stops at the water fountains. And she used the restroom only at lunchtime, when she knew it would be crowded.

At the end of the day, during silent reading time, Monica fell asleep on her desk. When the first bus bell jarred her awake, she looked around in confusion. Sunlight was streaming through the windows. And except for Janice Brown, who was watching her and pointing, most of the class was busy packing up. Monica began filling her backpack with books, hurrying so she wouldn't miss her bus.

"Monica?" Mr. Rossi called. "You're a car rider today. Your mother left a message in the office."

Monica could feel her heart pounding. Her mother never picked her up from school unless she had a doctor's appointment. Grateful for the end-of-day noise and confusion, Monica made her way to her teacher's desk.

"Mr. Rossi? Are you sure it was my mother who called?" Monica asked.

Mr. Rossi nodded. "Yes," he said quietly. "I double-checked with the secretary. I need to take some papers to the office after dismissal, though. Would you like me to walk down with you?"

Monica nodded. First she'd fallen asleep in class. Now she was afraid to walk down the hall of her own school by herself. What was happening to her?

After the last bus had been called, Mr. Rossi stood up. "Car riders and walkers? I have an errand to run. Why don't we get a head start?"

Monica walked down the hall with Erica, Jonathan, and Meghan, grateful that Mr. Rossi was only a few steps behind. When they reached the front doors of the school, she was relieved to see her mother's dark blue SUV. She turned and smiled at Mr. Rossi, then ran to the car, practically jumping into the front seat.

“Hi, Mom! This is a cool surprise! Or … not.”

Her mother’s eyes were red and swollen, and her face was blotchy. “Mom?”

Her mother sniffled, then took a deep breath. “I’m okay,” she said, though she looked anything *but* okay. “I wanted to give you more warning, that’s all.”

“Warning about what?”

Her mother pulled out of the parking lot and turned right. “Mom, our house is *that* way,” Monica said, pointing behind her. “You’re scaring me.”

“Honey, we have a stop to make. We’re meeting your father at the mall.”

“My father? No! I don’t want to meet him!”

“Honey, I have no choice. He wanted to pick you up from school, but my lawyer intervened. We’re meeting at the food court in the mall. My lawyer is meeting us there as well. We will both be there the whole time. If you want to be alone with your father, you may. But we are all staying in the food court, even if it’s at separate tables.”

“Why do we need to have a lawyer there?” Monica asked.

“I just feel better knowing that she’s there. Besides,” Mom said, smiling feebly, “she’ll help keep me on my best behavior.”

Monica had never seen her mother on anything but her best behavior, especially in public. She was one of the most dignified people Monica knew.

“Mom, are you all right?” Monica asked.

“I’m fine, honey. Shelley will keep me company. You just let us know what you need. We will sit with you at first. But if you want to be alone with your father, we will respect that and move to another table.”

“You won’t go far?” Monica asked.

“No.”

“Mom, I’m scared.”

“You don’t need to be,” her mother said. “He’s your father, after all. It’s about time you two met, don’t you think?”

“You don’t want this any more than I do,” Monica said.

Her mother took a deep breath. “No, Monica, I don’t. But he *is* your father and I don’t have any right to keep you away from him if he wants to see you. I will do everything I can to make this comfortable for you. That’s another reason Shelley is coming along. She can be objective about this. I can’t.”

The door to the mall loomed four parking spaces away. Monica flipped down the sun visor and looked into the mirror. She tried to coax her dark hair into place. She started to fan her eyes so he wouldn’t know she’d been crying, then stopped. *He should know*, she thought. *It’s his fault.*

She flipped the sun visor back up. Her mother was rolling down her window to speak with a tall, thin woman with salt-and-pepper hair.

“Hi, Victoria,” the woman said to Monica’s mother. “They’re here. Just inside the doors. You must be Monica,” she continued. “I’m Shelley Herman, your mom’s attorney.

“Who’s *they*?” Monica asked, “Isn’t it just *him*?”

“His attorney is with him,” Shelley said.

“Mom, do I have to do this?”

Her mother looked at Shelley. “How long do we have to stay?”

“Not very,” Shelley said. “But, we need to say more than *hello* and *good-bye.”*

“Don’t worry, honey. I will be right there with you,” Mom reassured her. “I’m not leaving the table unless you want me to.”

“Okay,” Monica said. “Let’s get this over with.”

As they approached the doors, Monica could see two men standing just inside the mall. One was slight, with wavy blond hair. He wore a gray suit and a red tie and carried a briefcase.

Beside him was a taller man with dark, close-cut hair. He wore a light blue polo shirt and khakis and held a pink gift bag in his hand. As they got closer, Monica could see a doll sticking out of the top of the bag. What? Was he kidding? She willed her expression back to neutral as they walked through the doors and into the mall.

The dark-haired man nodded at Monica's mother. "Victoria," he said. Then he focused his gaze on Monica. "You must be Monica," he said, his eyes tearing. "I'm Dr. Ted Lansky. I'm your father."

"Dr. Lansky is a neurosurgeon, Monica," the blond man said.

"It's nice to meet you," Monica managed to say.

"How about if we find a table?" Dr. Lansky asked. "Are you hungry?"

Monica shook her head, then looked at her mother.

"Victoria, would you care to join us?" he asked.

"I wouldn't have it any other way, Ted. Shelley will be joining us as well," She looked at the blond attorney. "Would you care to join us, Mr. … ?"

"Hawkins," he said, sticking out a well-manicured hand. "Melvin Hawkins."

Monica had no idea how her mother had summoned up so much poise, but she was charming and gracious throughout the entire ordeal. Dr. Lansky asked Monica about school, her hobbies, and her friends and seemed genuinely contrite about his gift being so embarrassingly inappropriate.

"I've missed so much of your life," he said. "I don't know much about twelve-year-old girls, but I'm willing to learn."

Monica tried to summon up the courage she'd had in her dreams to ask him why now? What had made him decide, after twelve years, that it was time to be a father?

"I'm really tired," she said instead, looking at her mother. "Can we go home now?"

Dr. Lansky stood and extended his hand. "Thank you for meeting with me, Monica. I hope we can get together again soon."

Monica shook his hand, and took the pink gift bag his attorney thrust into her other hand. "It was nice meeting you," she said.

Monica could feel him watching them all the way to the mall doors. So she had a father, after all. A doctor who bought dolls. Nothing had changed, but everything was different.

Chick Flicks And Porch Swings

(Coping With Parents' New Relationships)

SUMMARY:

Thomas has barely adjusted to his parents' divorce, and now both of his parents are dating. He doesn't understand how his parents can get along so well, yet still want to live apart and see other people.

POST-STORY DISCUSSION QUESTIONS:

Some of the following questions can be answered with a "yes" or "no." In these cases, the child giving an answer should explain his/her reasons.

1. When Thomas sees his mother getting ready for her date, why is he tempted to startle her so she has to redo her makeup?
2. Why does Thomas think it's "weird" that his parents can talk and laugh like old friends?
3. When Thomas's father meets Eric, he's friendly and polite. How do you think Thomas wanted him to react? Why?
4. Jeff thinks that Thomas gets upset when he sees his mother with someone other than his dad. Do you think Jeff is right? If he is, is Thomas wrong to feel this way?
5. Thomas asks why parents have to date. How would you answer that question?
6. Can divorced parents actually be friends?
7. How soon after a divorce should parents be allowed to date? Should kids meet all of the people their parents date?

Chick Flicks And Porch Swings

He was halfway up the stairs when he heard her humming. *Great,* Thomas thought, *just great.*

Sure enough, when he peeked into his mother's room, he saw her perched at the dressing table, carefully applying mascara. She was wearing the lavender silk robe his father had given her for Valentine's Day one year when they were still together. Her nails were painted a cherry red, and Thomas could tell they were still wet by the way she held her mascara wand. He was tempted to yell "Mom!" and push open the door. She would jump, and the wand would jerk. The mascara would go all over her face and she'd have to start her makeup again. Maybe even redo her nails. She might decide it wasn't worth the trouble to get all fancy again, and she'd stay home and play video games with him instead of going out.

He knocked softly on the door. “Mom?”

The humming stopped and she turned, revealing her partially made-up face. She looked like a weirdly glamorous pirate—one eye shadowed, mascara-ed, and lined and the other pale and neglected.

“Are you going out?” Thomas asked her.

“Yes,” his mother replied, a dreamy look in her eyes. “I’m going to dinner with Eric.”

“Oh. Well, I just came up to tell you I’m going for a run,” Thomas said.

“Don’t be long.” Her voice sounded vaguely annoyed. “Your father will be here soon to pick you up.”

“I’m going to Dad’s?”

“Yes, you’re going to Dad’s. Thomas, we talked about this last night. You’re twelve years old. I expect you to remember things for more than thirty seconds.”

“Sorry, Mom,” he muttered, running down the stairs and out of the house. He gave the porch swing a push as he ran by, then headed out to the sidewalk.

Thomas jogged past the houses on his street. *That’s it,* he thought. *Dump me on Dad so you can go out with Eric.*

His feet pounded the pavement. It wasn’t that he minded going to his dad’s. And he liked Eric. It was just that he and Mom had things down. Sort of a rhythm. Another adult would throw everything off.

“Hi, Tom,” came a familiar voice.

Thomas stopped short, almost running into Allie Cramer. A head taller than Thomas, with blonde hair that curled around her chin, Allie had been batting her blue eyes at him since fourth grade. She was cute and all, but a little too girly and made-up for his tastes.

“Hey, Allie,” Thomas replied.

“Going for a run?” she asked.

“Yeah, want to come?” Thomas asked, suppressing a grin. Sweat and Allie didn’t mix.

“Sure,” she said.

Thomas gulped, then coughed. “Actually, I’m almost finished. I have to be home in a few minutes to meet my dad.”

“Oh,” Allie’s shiny smile changed into a pout. “Maybe next time.”

“Oh, yeah. Maybe. See ya.”

Thomas sprinted away, continuing past the houses on Allie’s block, then veering off and running home through the park.

By the time he got home, his dad was there, sitting at the kitchen table. Thomas’s mother sat next to him. Her makeup was complete now, and a pale blue sun dress had replaced the lavender robe. Sitting next to Thomas’s father, her hand grazing his as they chatted and laughed like old friends, she looked as though she were on a date with him.

Weird, Thomas thought. *Totally weird.*

“Hey, Dad,” he called.

“Hi, Tom.” Dad looked at him and grinned. “I’d ask if you’re ready to go, but you sure don’t *smell* ready.”

“Are we going somewhere?” Thomas asked.

“Just out for pizza. Angela and Jeff are meeting us there.”

Angela’s was Dad’s “friend” and Jeff was her thirteen-year-old son. Thomas sighed, “I’ll get a shower.”

“Make it quick,” his mother said, annoyance creeping back into her voice.

Fifteen minutes later, Thomas was showered and changed. He ran downstairs, anxious to leave before Eric got there and his mother went all dreamy.

Thomas stopped on the bottom step. All of the adults, including Eric, were in the living room.

Thomas's father looked up. "Ready, Tom?" he asked. Then he stood and extended his hand to Eric. "Nice meeting you."

"You, too, Paul," Eric answered.

Thomas stared at them. *That was it? Nice to meet you? No lectures? No harsh words? No complaints about Eric dating his wife?*

"Thomas?" his mother said. She was standing beside him, her narrowed eyes belying her smile and telling him he'd zoned out again. "Eric said *hello."*

"Sorry, Mom. Hey, Eric. Uh, bye."

"Good night, honey," his mother said. "Have fun."

Thomas knew he should say, "You, too." But the truth was, he didn't really want his mother to have fun.

At the pizza place, Jeff and Thomas sat next to the jukebox. Their parents chose a booth by the door.

"It's just too weird, Jeff," Thomas said, taking another slice of pizza. "My dad's like Mr. Congeniality or something."

"What'd you expect him to do?" Jeff answered. "Punch the guy?"

"No, but shouldn't it bug him that my mom's going on a date with someone else?"

"Sounds like it bugs you," Jeff said, his mouth full of pizza. "You have to tell your mom."

"I can't tell my mother not to date."

"Don't tell her not to date, you doofus. Just tell her you hate it when you see her with someone other than your dad."

Thomas glanced at his father and Angela, sitting shoulder-to-shoulder, reading the menu. Angela's eyes had *the look.* Thomas had seen it in Allie's eyes when he'd asked her to run with him and in his mother's eyes when she'd told him she was going out with Eric. All of a sudden, Thomas felt sick.

"Did that work with your mom?" he asked Jeff.

Jeff stopped chewing. "No," he shrugged. "But that's just my mom."

After dinner, they went to Angela's. The adults watched a movie in the family room while Jeff and Thomas played video games in the basement.

How can he say they're just friends? Thomas thought, as he fired wildly at the aliens on the screen. *He's watching a chick flick! What's the matter with my parents?*

"Tom?" Jeff called, waving his hand in front of Thomas's face. "You've played this game before, right?"

Thomas stopped firing and squinted at the screen. He'd earned no points on his last turn, and now it was Jeff's turn again.

Thomas threw the controls on the sofa. "I'm going upstairs," he said.

"You really want to watch that movie?" Jeff asked, a disgusted look on his face.

"How can you sit here calmly shooting at aliens while our parents are upstairs watching a chick flick?"

Jeff shrugged. "My mom's a 'chick'. She watches those movies all the time. Video games are a form of survival around here."

"But my dad doesn't watch that stuff! He's an action-adventure guy. Why do parents have to date?"

"Do you really want me to answer that?" Jeff asked.

Thomas cringed. “Please don’t.”

“Tom, they’re just friends. At least so far.”

“But what happens when they realize they’re more than friends?” Thomas said.

“You’ll deal with it,” Jeff told him. “It could be worse, you know. My mom’s actually pretty cool.”

“I know. I like your mom.”

“She’s just not *your* mom.”

“No, that’s not it.” Thomas thought for a minute. “Sometimes when my parents are together, it seems like they really like each other. So it’s weird seeing them with anyone else. It’s all happening way too fast.”

The basement door opened. “Tom?” his dad called downstairs. “You ready to go?”

“Yeah,” he yelled back. “See ya, Jeff.”

“Later.”

Thomas hurried to the car, waving *good night* to Angela from the street so he wouldn’t have to see her eyes when she said *good night* to his dad on the front porch. Once Thomas was in the car, he slumped in his seat, scowling at the ceiling.

“Did you have fun?” Dad asked as he opened the car door.

“I guess.” Thomas sat up and looked at his father. “Doesn’t it bother you that Mom dates other men?” he asked.

Dad looked surprised. “Tom, your mother and I aren’t married any more. She’s allowed to date.”

“And that doesn’t bug you?”

"It used to," Dad admitted. "But it's nice to see her happy, and Eric seems okay."

"But he could wreck everything!"

"What exactly is he going to wreck by taking your mother out to dinner?" Dad asked.

His father just didn't get it. "Nothing. Forget it."

They were both quiet the rest of the way home. Thomas figured his dad was thinking about Angela. And if he was, Thomas didn't want to know. He thought back to their faces at the restaurant. Dad hadn't looked all dreamy and mushy, but he had looked happy. And Eric made his mom happy. So why was *he* so unhappy?

Thomas snapped out of his thoughts just in time to see the car pass his front porch. "Umm, Dad? That was the house," he said, turning around in his seat and pointing.

He froze. His mother and Eric were on the porch swing, sitting very close together. Eric had his arm around her shoulders. And his mom had *the look.*

Great. Thomas thought. *Just great.*

Brooklyn Blues

(Adjusting To Marital Separation)

SUMMARY:

Jacob and his father are spending the summer in Brooklyn, where Jacob's father, a rabbi, has been asked to help lead his childhood congregation. When Jacob's mother stays behind in Pennsylvania and his father registers him for school in New York, Jacob must face the fact that his family may be changing.

POST-STORY DISCUSSION QUESTIONS:

Some of the following questions can be answered with a "yes" or "no." In these cases, the child giving an answer should explain his/her reasons.

1. Why didn't Jacob's mother go to Brooklyn with him and his father?
2. Do you think Jacob likes having his father as a dad, rabbi, and principal? Would you like having your dad in all those roles?
3. Should Jacob get to choose whether he stays in Brooklyn or goes back to Pennsylvania? Why or why not?
4. Why do you think Jacob listened in on his father's phone call? Do you think what he did was right?
5. When Jacob's dad talks with his mom on the phone, Jacob says he's never heard his dad speak to her that way before. Why do you think Jacob's father used a different tone of voice? What do you think his voice sounded like?
6. Jacob's father says, "A wife should be with her husband." Do you agree?
7. What does Jacob's father mean when he says, "Sometimes our obligations conflict"?
8. Jacob's father says, "Your mother is very angry with me, and that makes it hard for her to come here." What does he mean? Do you think Jacob's mother still loves Jacob's father?
9. Do you think Jacob's parents will get a divorce? Why or why not?

Brooklyn Blues

My name is Jacob Aaron Asher. I live in Brooklyn, New York. At least I do for now. My dad usually works as a rabbi at Bartlett College in Lewisville, Pennsylvania. But last May, the rabbi at the temple my dad went to when he was a kid had a stroke. His wife asked my grandma if Dad could come to Brooklyn and fill in until Rabbi Weintraub got better. Dad said *yes* right away. You see, Rabbi Weintraub inspired my dad to become a rabbi in the first place.

I didn't really mind coming here. We're staying at my grandparents' house, and my friend, Alan Steinman, lives downstairs. I usually only get to see him when we visit Gram and Grandpa, but being here for the summer means that I get to hang out with him every day. I've known him ever since we were little kids, because my parents and I lived in Brooklyn until I was two years old.

The only trouble with being in Brooklyn is that I miss my mom. She's vice-president of an advertising agency in Lewisville. She started the business with a friend of hers when both of them got downsized from a big company. Because it's just the two of them, they're really busy. They have to go on trips and go to meetings whenever clients want them. It's good for business, but bad for me. It seems like every time she's supposed to visit us, something happens with work and she can't come. Dad says we can't go to see her because of his responsibilities here, and Rabbi Weintraub's recovery is taking way longer than anybody thought it would. Gram says that's because he knows his congregation's in good hands, so he can take his time.

But school starts next week. Dad took a leave of absence from the college for the fall semester so we could stay here. He even enrolled me in the Jewish Day School, but I don't want to go there. For starters, my dad's the acting principal while Rav Weintraub is recovering. I'm a fifth grader, so if we were at home, I'd be one of the oldest kids in the school. But here, the school goes up to sixth grade. Besides, the school's really tiny and far away from my mom and all of my friends except Alan. And I'm starting to wonder if something's going on with my parents.

"Jakie!"

I sit up really fast and get a strange dizzy feeling in my head. "What's up, Gram?"

"I've been calling you. Alan is downstairs waiting for you."

"Sorry, Gram! I'll be right down."

I slide off the bed, grab my sneakers, and run downstairs.

"Hey, Alan," I say.

"Hey, yourself," Alan replies. "Get your bike. They finished the mowing at school."

"So … "

"All the equipment's gone! We have the whole parking lot to ride in!"

"Gimme a minute to get my bike helmet. See ya, Gram!" I yell.

Gram comes out of the kitchen, her hands on her hips and her apron dusted with flour. "And where do you think you're going?"

"To the school. I'll be back in time to set the table."

"Okay, Jakie," Gram says. When she comes over to give me a kiss, I notice she smells like cinnamon. "Be careful."

"It's okay, Mrs. Asher," Alan reassures her. "We can't get into too much trouble. After all, Rav Asher's in charge of the school."

Gram smiles. "Have fun, boys," she tells us.

"Yeah, fun," I mutter as we go down the front steps.

"What's with you?" Alan asks. "Don't you want to see the school?"

"I'm not even sure I'm staying."

"What do you mean? School starts next week. Of course you're staying."

"Yeah, but if I go back to Pennsylvania with my mom … "

"Jake, when's the last time you saw your mom?"

"I talked with her on the phone … "

"No," Alan insists. "When's the last time you *saw* her?"

"Umm … Fourth of July?"

"That was two months ago! Jake, you said it yourself. She's busy. Really busy. Face facts," Alan grins. "You're stuck with me. Besides, the Day School's pretty good. And I'm sure your dad will be more fun than Rav Weintraub. Your dad's a lot younger and cooler."

"Easy for you to say," I grumble. "Your dad's just your dad. He's not your rabbi and your principal, too."

At the school, we find the parking lot empty but the front door open. We park our bikes and walk in, curious to see what's going on. The lobby smells like varnish and chalk dust, even though no one has written on the boards in three months.

We're barely inside when the office door swings open and Dad walks out. He has gray hair and a gray beard, even though he's only 45. But today his face looks gray, too, and the bounce that's usually in his step is completely gone.

"Hello, boys," he says, trying to smile but failing miserably.

"Hi, Rav Asher," Alan replies, standing a bit taller.

"Hey, Dad. What's up?"

"I'm afraid I've had some bad news. Rabbi Weintraub has had another stroke."

Alan turns white and slides into a sitting position on the floor.

I look from Alan to my dad. "Are you all right?" I say, not sure if I'm asking Alan or my dad.

Alan nods, and so does Dad. "Mrs. Weintraub is having a difficult time, though," Dad tells us.

"But Rabbi Weintraub will be okay, right?" I ask.

Dad shrugs, "He's expected to improve. But no one knows for sure if he'll be able to speak or walk again."

"So we could be here a lot longer?" I ask, suddenly missing Pennsylvania immensely.

"Yes."

"I don't want to stay here!"

The force of my words surprises both of us and Dad hesitates a moment before he speaks. His words are quiet, but his eyes are hard. "I'm afraid that isn't your decision, Jacob. Nice to see you, Alan," Dad says, walking back into his office.

Alan and I ride our bikes for the rest of the afternoon. We're both worried about Rabbi Weintraub, and I'm worried about never seeing my mom again.

At home, dinner is solemn. Gram must have heard the news, because it looks like a holiday meal. We have appetizers, roast chicken, stuffing, mashed potatoes, corn, green beans, carrots, rolls, and a choice of desserts. I guess Gram figures if we're busy eating, we can't talk about Rabbi Weintraub.

After dinner, Dad excuses himself. I know he's going upstairs to call Mom so I won't hear his phone conversation. This is one call I definitely don't want to miss. When Grandpa goes into the bathroom and Gram starts the dishes, I know this is my chance. I clear the rest of the dirty dishes, then tiptoe upstairs.

The phone is in my grandparents' bedroom. I slide down the wall at the top of the steps, placing my ear next to the partially open bedroom door.

"Andrea, I realize you have clients," my dad is saying, "but can't you conduct some of your business via e-mail? And you can certainly find clients in Brooklyn."

I've never heard my dad speak to my mom in that tone before. He's not yelling, but I can tell he's angry.

"He misses you," I hear Dad say, "and he wonders why he can't come back to his old school. You aren't the only one who is having difficulty with this separation."

Separation? Does he mean *separation,* like in divorce?

"Yes, maybe we should," Dad says.

Should? Should what?

"No, Andrea, I cannot come back now. Your business is more easily conducted from here than mine is from there. And a wife should be with her husband."

"Jakie!"

I jump up and look around before I realize Gram is calling me from the kitchen. I run downstairs, careful to move quickly but quietly so she won't know where I've been. Through the foyer, through the living room and dining room, and into the kitchen.

"Yes, Gram."

"There you are! Take out the garbage, please."

"Sure, Gram."

When I run down the stoop to put the garbage out front, I nearly run over Alan, who is sitting on the steps.

"Man, am I glad to see you," I tell him after I put the trash on the curb. "I think my dad just had a phone fight with my mom."

Alan just laughs. "My parents have those all the time. Once my mom didn't speak to my dad for a whole week because of something he said during a phone fight. My brother and I got away with all kinds of stuff that week."

"But this one sounded bad, Alan."

The door opens behind us and Dad calls me in. I tell Alan I'll see him tomorrow and follow my dad inside.

"Sit down, Jacob," Dad says as soon as I close the door. "It looks as though we're going to be here longer than we expected. For business reasons, your mother is unable join us and, for similar reasons, I am unable to say when I can go back to Pennsylvania. I feel an obligation to stay here and make sure things are in good hands, particularly since Rabbi Weintraub has a long recovery ahead of him."

"What about Mom? Don't you feel an obligation to her?"

"Of course I do, Jacob," Dad replies in a voice that is softer than I expected, "but sometimes our obligations conflict."

"Do you still love each other?"

"Yes, we do, and we both love you. It's just that our lives seem to be taking different paths now and we both feel that we need to follow those paths."

"Are you getting a divorce?"

"I hope it won't come to that."

"Will I get to see Mom?"

"Of course you will," Dad answers. "Why would you even ask me that?"

I hesitate. "Well ... she's been so busy this summer. It's almost like she doesn't want to see us."

Dad takes off his glasses and rubs his eyes. "Jacob, your mother is very angry with me, and that makes it hard for her to come here. But of course she wants to see you."

"Then why doesn't she come get me?"

"Son, you know my schedule is more predictable than your mother's. And if I have an emergency at work and can't be here, at least Gram and Grandpa can. If you went back home, you'd be spending a lot of time with a babysitter. Here, you're with family."

"Will we ever be a family again? You and Mom and I?"

"Your mother and I have a lot to work out, and I can't predict the future. For now, you'll stay here with your grandparents and me, and your mother will stay in Lewisville. We'll work out a schedule of visits so that you can see your mother as often as possible."

I must look as though I don't believe him, because after a pause, he adds, "And we'll both do our best to keep our work schedules from interfering with those visits."

"So I'll go to school here, and you'll be my principal?"

"I don't expect that to be a problem, Jacob. As long as you behave yourself, you won't have to see your principal at all." His voice softens, "Why don't you go see if Alan is still out on the stoop? I have to speak with your grandparents."

Dad heads for the living room and I go to the front door and fling it open. Alan's gone, but I go out and sit on the stoop anyway, trying to focus on the sky as the sun sets behind the brownstones across the street. *So I'm a New Yorker, again. New school. New friends. But what will happen to my old family?*